Slave to the Clock, Master of Time

Slave to the Clock, Master of Time

Sean McLoughney

Chartered Accountants Ireland

First published in 2008
Reprinted in 2012 by
Chartered Accountants Ireland
Chartered Accountants House
47–49 Pearse Street
Dublin 2
www.charteredaccountants.ie

ISBN: 9780903854085

Typeset by Marsha Swan
Printed and bound by CPI Group (UK) Ltd, Croydon, CR0 4YY

CONTENTS

ACKNOWLEDGEMENTS

When I first put this project forward to Kieran Lyons, he enthusiastically told me to go off and write the book and to enjoy the experience. At four o'clock in the morning when I reached that point when I had to decide whether the best use of my time was to catch a few hours of sleep before heading off to work or to finish a chapter, I wondered if this is what Kieran had meant when he said 'enjoy the experience'.

Writing a book is a solitary exercise, which requires the backing and support of many people. I would like to thank all of those who have helped and encouraged me throughout this project. I owe an enormous debt of gratitude to Marsha Swan for bringing this book alive through her editing and design. Agnieszka Pobedynska kept the project moving along and ensured that we met our deadline, which is just as well considering the subject matter. I would also like to thank Barry Brophy for encouraging me to stop talking about writing a book and to start writing it.

I would especially like to thank Carol for her support and encouragement and a very big thank you to Alex and Rachel for being the best two girls in the world.

Lastly, I would like to thank all those who contributed to the book through their tips, stories, words of praise and encouragement and their enthusiasm for the project. Kieran, many thanks for all your help and words of wisdom and, yes, I did enjoy the experience.

MYTH NO. I
TIME MANAGEMENT IS ABOUT MANAGING TIME

YOU NEED TO MANAGE YOUR TIME BETTER

'John, my office, now!' – an order relayed in a tone John had become accustomed to, but at the same time feared. Those four simple words echoing around the office alerted John to the fact that his boss, Alex, wasn't happy. The sudden realisation of the consequences of another dreaded deadline passing dominated his thoughts. How would he explain his tardiness this time? Maybe she would be understanding and realise it wasn't entirely his fault. Maybe the Sales Director would come to his aid and take the blame. Maybe she was moving the deadline to a more realistic hour. John, ever the optimist, was mistaken if he ever truly believed his summons to her office was for anything other than another tongue-lashing.

John was a nice, amiable sort of guy who worked very hard. Always willing to stay late in order to finish the work, John had developed a reputation amongst his peers as being the guy to help others with their workload. As a result, many of his less-than-scrupulous colleagues would pass on their work to him as they knew he would never say no. As they left for home John would be seen working away at his desk, which was piled high with unfinished reports and incomplete files. His boss didn't see this side of John; all she was aware of was his inability to complete the reports she needed on time, and that his colleagues didn't seem to have the same problem.

Alex would regularly be heard saying, 'Where are this week's sales figures? You know I need them for the board meeting today. How many times do I have to remind you that the deadline for your report is 3:00,

'Don't wait. The time will never be just right.'

Napoleon Hill

not 5:30? We live by deadlines. You have to get on top of your workload and start delivering. Either get in earlier or skip lunch or something because you can't be late every week with these figures. Don't you realise how important your report is? We're all waiting on it; you're making me look bad.'

'But the sales guys haven't given them to me yet; they keep telling me they can't give the figures to me until 4:00,' John would reply half-heartedly, knowing Alex wasn't interested in his explanation.

'Excuses I don't need, figures I do need, and need them now. Get help from someone if you're unable to get the report finished on time.' Then she would finish the dressing down with the career-going-nowhere line, 'If you can't manage your time effectively, I can't see you ever managing a team. If you can't meet deadlines, how would you ensure that your team would meet theirs? You're a big disappointment; I don't know what to do with you. Maybe you should go on a time management course and see if that will work – I want to see a big improvement.'

Today when he left her office with those words ringing in his ear John realised he had become a 'slave to the clock'. Like most people, he wished there were more hours in the day so he could complete his reports on time. He was weighed down with work, which was piling up on his desk. He really wanted to move his deadlines and be free of the constant, embarrassing telling-offs from his boss. Unfortunately he could see no way of escaping his deadline shackles. He accepted that they were an essential part of his job. Despair and hopelessness engulfed him as he sat at his desk and thought about his next move. How could he improve his situation? Would he ever enjoy his job again? Would a time management course really help?

Can you relate to John?

Have you ever found yourself in that unenviable position where you felt that your job made you a slave to the clock? Have you ever felt you couldn't cope with your workload? Have you ever attended a time management training course and believed you were sent as a punishment or because you were an ineffective worker? Have you ever read a time management book and agreed with the principles discussed, but felt you couldn't apply them? Have you ever been given a great time management tip and dismissed it, believing it was great in theory but couldn't work in practice, particularly for you? Have you ever used the excuse, 'If only I'd more time I would have got it finished'? Or, 'I would love to help you on the committee if only I had the time'? Are you constantly battling the clock to meet demanding deadlines, to get to the meeting on time, or to struggle home to pick up the children from school or attend some after-school activity? If these situations resonate with you, then you are in the majority. Being a slave to the clock is now reaching endemic proportions.

Still getting it wrong

Despite the fact that there have been thousands of books and articles written on the subject, millions of euro spent on cutting-edge technology to help overburdened workers complete their excessive workloads, and training courses that run every day on time management, many people are no better at it today than their colleagues were 20 or 30 years ago. In fact, a recent report stated that 75 per cent of professional people struggle with their time management skills.

It is not just at the workplace that people struggle with managing their time. When you finally get home after spending a hectic day being tortured by the clock, you are then challenged with cramming a day's home activities into the five or so remaining hours. The house needs your tender care, clothes scream out to be washed and ironed, the grass requires a good haircut, the paintwork is aching for a makeover, and the list goes on. Add children, spouses or pets into the equation and the need for mastering time becomes not an ambition but an essential requirement. People who are slaves to the clock can only dream about living the life they want, while masters of their time live the life of their dreams. Nelson Mandela puts it: 'There is no passion to be found playing small – in settling for a life that is less than the one you are capable of living.' The great thing about time management is that everyone can be a true master of their time if they really want to.

If mastering your time is an indispensable ingredient in having a rewarding life, then why do so many people get it wrong? According to R. Alec Mackenzie in *The Time Trap: The Classic Book on Time Management*, the reason is simple: most articles, books, seminars, toolkits and trainers focus on the symptoms of poor time management instead of the root cause, which is people. Therefore common symptoms such as missed deadlines, badly managed workloads and lack of task-planning are typically solved by a beleaguered boss telling a frustrated worker to improve their time management skills, which is usually followed by an order to attend a course if the situation doesn't improve. This quick fix often provides people with limited, short-term success. However, such remedies don't solve the real

When was the last time you did one of the following?

- Spent quality time on yourself
- Took up a new hobby
- Increased your leisure time
- Spent as much time as you wanted with your loved ones
- Calculated the time you spend on the things that mean the most to you
- Left work early because you had nothing else to do that day
- Did absolutely nothing and not felt guilty about it

problem, and often lead to further failure and frustration.

Stephen Covey, in his book *First Things First*, talks about the fourth generation of time management. The first three generations looked at ways to be more efficient and effective. They are about tips and techniques. In the fourth generation, Covey believes in managing time based on your values. Masters of time continually add value to their lives and those that are important to them. They align their values to their work life. They manage themselves and those around them and let time take care of itself.

WHAT IS TIME MANAGEMENT?

When people are asked this question they regularly give the obvious answer, that it is about a person's ability to manage and control time. Traditionally, time management experts focused on improving a person's efficiency through time management skills. It was about developing processes such as diary planners and to-do lists, which could ensure daily tasks are completed on time. They took the view that all people needed to do to improve their productivity was to learn a few time management techniques or tricks.

Unfortunately, such a simple view often leads to disappointment, frustration due to an unrealistic understanding of what time management can achieve, and finally a condemnation of what time management stands for. Being efficient is not the same as being effective. Efficient people get things done, whereas effective people get the right things done. Time management is more than just planning and organising your tasks in order to complete them as quickly as possible. It is a philosophy on how you manage your life, and doing the things you believe are important. The notion that traditional time management tips are the answer to your problems is a recipe for failure. The key is not the tips, but how you use the tips.

Time cannot be managed
Hectic work schedules, challenging deadlines, lack of human resources and tightening budgets have given the modern workplace many new problems, none more difficult than the lack of time. People are under

increasing pressure to achieve more and more from every day. A desire for efficiency and effectiveness, coupled with other people's expectations, means the vast majority of people are now slaves to the clock. Lives revolve around deadlines, appointments, and constant clock-watching to see if you will make your next meeting on time. Many people believe that time management is about ensuring that every minute of every day is accounted for and used productively. Such slavery needs a crusader (you) who will fight for freedom and debunk the many myths now associated with time management.

The skill of time management is not about managing time. It is more complex. You cannot create more time if you run short – there will always be 24 hours in a day, 168 hours in a week. You cannot motivate time either – it will move at the same pace today as it did yesterday and as it will tomorrow. You cannot reason with time as it will march on relentlessly whether you are ready or not. You cannot save up some time today and use it later in the month. Time, unlike people, cannot be managed.

The best way to win the battle against the shackles of the chronometer and achieve what you want from your day is to master your time. There is a wealth of knowledge available to improve how you use your time; however, Douglas Adams once said, 'Human beings, who are almost unique in having the ability to learn from the experience of others, are also remarkable for their apparent disinclination to do so.' Learning from past mistakes and converting the knowledge into action are essential components in your quest to become a true master of time. There is no need to seek out new tricks, tips or techniques – instead concentrate on successful implementation of the techniques you already know.

View time management as a core business and personal management skill, with its main principles built around managing yourself and the people around you. These management skills are necessary for success; they help to identify and focus on the activities that give you the greatest return for your time. Effective time management skills will ensure that you are more productive, efficient and work in an environment that is less stressful and more success-orientated. It is about enjoying your work and life and having time to be who you want to be and do what you want to do.

Business and personal management skills

To self-manage and manage other people effectively requires a comprehensive understanding of fundamental management skills. Skills such as planning, organising and controlling have been around since the early days of management theory. Theorists such as Henri Fayol and, later, Peter Drucker explained that it is the function of managers to set objectives and then have a strategy to achieve them. These objectives are best attained when broken down into smaller, manageable tasks. Once you know what you have to do, a manager's function is then to use the resources available and get the task completed.

The skills and techniques in this book are the same skills you use on a daily basis when you manage and interact with people. In addition to the traditional management skills of planning and organising, which help you to use your time more efficiently and effectively, you must also use the broader skills of leadership. Skills such as influencing decision-making, disciplining and dealing with different personalities are essential to becoming a master of time. Your leadership skills will help you to create a vision for your future and provide you with the determination and motivation to turn your vision into reality. Your leadership skills are the difference between being a slave to the clock and a master of your time. People will find some of the skills discussed easy to apply, while others will require work, practice and persistence. The key to success for top performers is that they invest their time wisely. It is now time to take responsibility for how you use your time.

'Success on any major scale requires you to accept responsibility… in the final analysis, the one quality that all successful people have… is the ability to take on responsibility.'
Michael Korda

Building a framework to manage yourself

To help put a framework on the skills required to manage yourself, consider the management functions put forward by French industrialist Henri Fayol in the early 1900s and apply them to your time management strategy. Fayol based his theory around the following functions:

Planning
Organising
Controlling
Commanding
Co-ordinating
Forecasting

These business management principles can be adapted to form a framework to help you establish a strategy for turning your vision into your way of managing your life. Some key leadership skills will also be added to Fayol's principles, which will provide you with your blueprint for success. All of these skills can be mastered by you.

Management	Leadership	Comment
Planning	Strategic thinking	This involves determining your key goals for the day/week/month/year. Adding-value lists Be SMARTER Best time of the day
Organising	Decision-making	Establishing and prioritising the tasks that need to be performed in order to achieve the goals on time and to the agreed standard. Prioritise your tasks against your role and deadlines Differentiate between urgent and important Consider expectations of your boss and organisation
Controlling	Discipline	Measuring how your time is spent will ensure that your output is in accordance with your plans. Time-audit log Valued interruptions vs. non-value interruptions Focus on what you can control
Commanding	Communicating	Stay in charge of your time. You need to manage yourself and those around you. Managing different personalities Influencing people Be assertive and learn to say no
Co-ordinating	Inspiring	Bring it all together and remain focused and persistent. Checklists – are you doing the right things? Action plan – mapping your journey 24-hour rule – get started now
Forecasting	Visionary	How you need to use your time in the future. Desired position Using your time like a master Identifying time blockages

Master your time

Write one great time management tip you've come across that is easy to implement.

It's about managing behaviours

There are countless time management tips people have been sharing with one another for decades. Most have been around a long time and have been proven to work for some people. The great time management tip you have written in your 'Master Your Time' file should be easy to implement. Therefore there is no reason to prevent you from benefiting from this tip straight away. This will give you a quick win, but unfortunately also a false sense that becoming a master of your time is easy. One of the rules written by legendary football coach Vince Lombardi in a book about his career entitled *What it Takes to Be #1* is, 'Don't buy the myth of the overnight success. Invest in your talent.' Improving your ability to manage yourself will take time and persistence as old time management habits are sometimes hard to break. Your old bad habits need to be weeded out ruthlessly and new habits and beliefs grown with the same dedication and care as a gardener grows prize-winning orchids.

Most articles written about time management and training programmes delivered on the same subject centre around the tools and techniques used to improve your time management skills. While they have their place, they alone will not improve how you use your time. They may achieve some short-term success but rarely long-term change. The cornerstone of successfully mastering your time is built around your mindset, how you use these tools and your desire to improve. This requires a long-term strategy and commitment to investing in your talent. It will be hard work at first but, to borrow a sport cliché, 'No pain, no gain.'

A major stumbling block to becoming a master of your time, whether it is through developing new ideas or updating existing time management principles, is attitude. The wrong attitude will inhibit your progress towards implementing your vision. Attitude alone can keep you enslaved to the clock. It can prevent you from unlearning old ways and habits that served you devotedly over many years. According to Dr Costas Karageorghis, an accredited sport and exercise psychologist, the state of mind of top performing athletes is an important component in achieving a winning performance. Talent alone is no guarantee for success. Similarly, knowing about the tools and techniques of time management is no guarantee that you will use them wisely or effectively. Some people have attended time management courses and read many books on the subject, but are still slaves to the clock. To be successful you must have a positive mindset and a belief that you can master your time. You must be prepared to put in the hard yards and break free from your comfort zone. You must be committed to change and the philosophy of being a master of your time. Being excellent requires constant development, analysing every part of your performance and patiently making small changes as required. Changes will take place, not overnight, but over time. Be brave and persistent; the rewards are worth the effort.

Make a decision

How much time will you waste today through indecision? Is it 15 minutes, 30 minutes, an hour or even longer? It would probably shock you if you quantified how much time you waste thinking about making decisions. The ability to make good decisions will transform the way you use your time. Tom Peters and Robert Waterman, after examining 40 of Fortune's top 500 performing companies in their book *In Search of Excellence*, found that there were eight common themes responsible for their success. The first theme was 'a bias for action', where organisations made active decisions. Successful companies took action as quickly as possible and then analysed the results and made changes if necessary.

Before you read another page it is now time to make an important decision. You need to decide if you truly want to become a master of your time. If the answer is yes then you must take responsibility for your decision and review all the options available to you. You are now responsible for your strategy and action plan, and for the consequences of your actions (or inaction), which means you can change your strategy if required. You are also responsible for your time management goals and eventual success.

Develop your strategy

A critical step towards becoming a liberated master of your time is to set your 'best way to use my time' goal. This goal is a driving force behind your successful voyage to freedom and turning your vision into the way you manage your life. Before you write out your goal, try to figure out why you want to embark on this journey as it will help you decide on the best course of action. Close your eyes and picture what your successful outcome will look like. Imagine it, feel it and get ready to live it. Be inspired and ready for success.

The following steps can guide you in writing a clear and rewarding 'best way to use my time' goal:

'Opportunity is missed by most people because it is dressed in overalls and looks like work.'
Thomas Edison

Mastering your winning mindset for improving how you use your time requires a well-thought-out strategy that includes setting goals and targets. Top athletes, like Tiger Woods, set an explicit goal of getting much better at what they do. They constantly challenge themselves to find ways of improving and getting more out of their performance. They have a clear vision of what they need to achieve and how they will achieve their success. They never settle for being less than what they can be. Being a top performer in the business world requires the same focused mindset and desire, the same attitude towards risk and the bravery to learn from everyone.

'We are the creative force of our life, and through our own decisions rather than our conditions, if we carefully learn to do certain things, we can accomplish those goals.'
Stephen Covey

The process of describing your desired position can be challenging and it often raises some important issues that need to be confronted. To really improve how you use your time, you need to be totally honest with yourself. Some of the key questions you might ask yourself that can help with this process are:

- Am I happy with the way I currently use my time?
- Are my boss/colleagues happy with the way I currently use my time?
- Am I really interested and committed to improving how I use my time?
- What will I achieve if I improve the way I use my time?
- What are the key indicators that will show my improvement?
- What changes would I make to how I currently spend my time?
- What is the primary benefit to me, my boss and my organisation if I improve how I use my time?

Step 1: Your vision

Alexander Graham Bell said: 'Concentrate all your thoughts upon the work at hand. The sun's rays do not burn until brought to a focus.' Describe in detail your desired position. Think big and positively. In *Golf Is Not a Game of Perfect* Dr Bob Rotella, a renowned sports psychologist and performance coach, talks about achieving great things through thinking big. He says, 'A person with great dreams can achieve great things. A person with small dreams, or a person without the confidence to pursue his or her dreams, has consigned himself or herself to a life of frustration and mediocrity.'

A clear vision of how you would prefer to use your time and the benefits that mastery of your time will give you will become your motivation and inspiration to succeed. For example, your desired position could be to leave your workplace on time at least three days a week, or to spend one hour per week developing your career, or to have a 'chill out family day' once a month without feeling guilty or checking your message-minder. Maybe your desired position is to complete your entire task list on a daily basis or to spend less time at routine, non-productive meetings. Perhaps spending more quality time with loved ones or pursuing your hobbies is the dream that propels your need to master your time.

Whatever your desired position is, you need to visualise it clearly. Sit down in a quiet room and close your eyes. Picture how you would like to use your time. Champion sports people use visualisation as part of their routine in the lead-up to significant events. It allows them to focus on their goal and to eliminate any distractions or barriers. This single-mindedness gives them the edge in their pursuit of peak performance.

Step 2: Write out your goals

Achieving important goals can be a daunting prospect for people. They imagine it to be harder than it actually is. 'It always seems impossible until it's done,' Nelson Mandela said. A simple but effective way to bring clarity to your goal is to write it out using the SMARTER Way Goal Setting System™: When you set yourself a task, goal or job to do, there are two elements that determine whether you are successful – a clear understanding of the goal and the motivation to achieve it. The SMARTER Way Goal Setting System™ is a great technique to use to achieve important results.

People are often too vague when outlining their goals, especially their time management goals. You must get yourself excited about completing your goals, otherwise there is a distinct possibility that procrastination will take root. It is also important that you see your reward, what's in it for you. This system will ensure you have a clear understanding of what you would like to achieve and the motivation to remain persistent.

The SMARTER Way Goal Setting System™ can be used as follows:

S	Specific
M	Measurable
A	Achievable
R	Relevant
T	Timeframe
E	Exciting
R	Reward

Specific. People often set career and personal goals that are simply too vague. 'I want an exciting job,' or, 'I want to improve my time management skills,' are goals that are hard to determine, whether you have achieved them or not. There are no goalposts, so how do you know if you have scored? However, if you re-word your goal to, 'I want to complete my sales report by 3:00 every Friday,' you now have a specific time management goal. Writing a clear goal will mean that you cannot distort the result. A specific goal shows that you either succeeded or you need to try harder. It concentrates the mind on focusing on the result.

Measurable. Winning goals need to have some form of measurement, like the old saying, 'What gets measured gets done.' Incorporating a clear measurement in your written goal will make it easier to see if you have hit your intended target. The measure should be linked to the specific part of your goal. 'I want to reduce by 20 per cent the number of trivial interruptions that I get every day,' is a goal with a definite measurement. You can also break down the overall measurement into smaller chunks, which will make it easier to achieve. These smaller targets can become benchmarks or progress signs.

Achievable. Your goals should stretch but not break you. The success or failure of your goals can often be determined by the fact that the goal was unrealistic in the first place. Naïve goals set you up to fail and, as a result, you run the risk of giving up before you even start. Equally,

'We cannot control life's difficult moments but we can choose to make life less difficult. We cannot control the negative atmosphere of the world, but we can control the atmosphere of our minds. Too often we try to choose and control things we cannot. Too seldom we choose to control what we can – our attitude.'

John Maxwell

if your goal is too easy, chances are it hasn't brought you any closer to being a true master of your time.

Your goal should force you out of any comfort zone you've fallen into. Try an idea that is challenging and will make a significant difference to how you use your time. Maintain a positive attitude towards achieving your goal.

Relevant. Avoid setting goals that aren't relevant to improving how you use your time. Relevant goals will ensure that all of your effort is devoted towards achieving your vision of 'perfect day'. Do not waste time on goals that will not move you towards your long-term objective. The relevance of your goal should be aligned to your motivation and inspiration to improve.

Timeframe. There is nothing like an impending deadline to concentrate the mind and body. People think and talk about how they wished they had more time to spend doing what they would like to do rather than the things that are imposed on them. They also bemoan the fact there aren't enough hours in the day to complete all of their tasks.

Most people never take action to implement their goal to change how they use their time because they don't set deadlines. As a result there is never a sense of urgency. Procrastination takes hold. Therefore, set realistic but challenging timeframes. Make them too short and you will become disillusioned because you will feel you're not progressing as quickly as you had hoped. In contrast, if you make the timeframe too long, you will waste a lot of time waiting for things to happen.

Decide on your starting date and calculate your finish date. Estimate how long each task will take to complete, allowing for interruptions. Include some milestones to help you track your progress and ensure you're on schedule to complete your goal on time.

Exciting. Make sure your goal is full of Es: excitement, enthusiasm, energy and enjoyment. Write out why your goal is exciting – so exciting that failure is not an option. Bring passion to your desire to achieve your goal. Energise those around you with your enthusiasm for success. Ensure your colleagues are also excited about your wish to improve your use of time.

Every day you should be excited about moving closer to your vision of a 'perfect day'. Talk enthusiastically about your goal; focus on why you want to achieve this goal of mastering your time. Make sure your energy levels are high as this will drive you forward. Finally, enjoy the journey – this is your goal, your time, your success.

Reward. What will you achieve as a result of completing this goal? List the many benefits achieving your goal will bring you, your boss and your organisation, as this list will improve your motivation to be successful.

Add incentives to your journey so that you can maintain your drive throughout your progress to peak performance. Achieving challenging goals isn't easy. It requires dedication, perseverance and a real desire to improve. If your reward is big enough you will ensure there are no barriers to your success.

Visualising and writing out your goals will become the lifeblood of your journey to mastering your time. While the SMART part of a goal gives you a clear understanding of what you have to do and the timeframe within which you will achieve your goal, the final ER part is the motivational drive behind your goal. It gives you the reason why you want to improve how you use your time.

Achieving outstanding results is based on your ability to be excited and enthused about your goals and to clearly understand what your rewards are. Why you want to improve your time management skills and what's in it for you are the two key questions that you must answer honestly. The answers will help you to get back on track if your plan starts to unravel or you become despondent or lose interest. Champions have a clear vision of their goal. How they achieve the goal might change but their goal remains fixed in their mind; this positive mindset shouldn't waiver.

Using the SMARTER Way Goal Setting System™ will transform your time management goals into desirable and attainable tasks. This system will convert the wishing into wanting and then into achieving. It will move you from thinking about change to making change happen for you.

Writing out your goal will increase your chances of success. A study on goal-setting sponsored by the Ford Foundation found that only 10 per cent of Americans had clearly defined goals, and 7 out of 10 of these achieved their goals only half the time. Three per cent of people, however, achieved their goals 89 per cent of the time. The reason for the high success rate is that they wrote down their goals.

These are just a few of the benefits you will experience from using the SMARTER Way Goal Setting System™:

- It will get you started
- It will give you a clear understanding as to why you want to improve
- It will help you get what you really want from your day
- It will keep you motivated and focused
- It will clearly state your rewards
- It will build persistence, which help you overcome barriers
- It will give you the edge
- It will focus you to achieving peak performance

Master your time

Use the SMARTER Way Goal Setting System™ to outline what you are going to achieve by the end of this book:

S

M

A

R

T

E

R

To illustrate how the SMARTER Way Goal Setting System™ works, look at how John can put it into action.

S	will complete my sales report by the deadline as agreed with Alex
M	98 per cent success rate will be acceptable
A	average standard in the department is 95 per cent so this improvement achievable
R	compiling sales reports is a key function of my job
T	month end for the first six months of the year
E	able to leave the office on time
	less stress as deadlines approach each week
	happiness as no longer letting people down by missing deadlines
R	reduces conflict with boss
	improves career prospects
	respect from peers and boss

Step 3: Map the map

Now that you have outlined your desired position and have written the SMARTER goals required to transform your vision into reality, you are now ready to focus on how to get there. Success doesn't happen by chance or luck – you need to plan for it. As Louis Pasteur remarked, 'Luck favours the prepared mind.'

If you are preparing for a journey to a town or city you haven't visited before, chances are you will either buy or borrow a map. You will choose the best route and calculate how long it will take you to get there. Why? The reason is simple; you set off on your journey full of enthusiasm and energy. You're excited about visiting somewhere different. Everyone has told you it is a great place to visit. About an hour into your journey, you meet a fork in the road and there is no signpost. Which road do you take? If you have a map, the decision is easy; if you haven't, you could take the wrong road and never reach the destination you have dreamt about for so long. The same principles apply to achieving your time management goals.

Stephen Covey, in his book *The Seven Habits of Highly Effective People*, takes this rule a step further. He says to 'begin with the end in mind', which is based on the principle that all things are created twice.

Firstly, you imagine it or think about an idea, and then secondly you create or build it. He gives the example of starting a business:

> If you want to have a successful enterprise, you clearly define what you're trying to accomplish. You carefully think through the product or service you want to provide in terms of your market target, then you organise all the elements – financial, research and development, operations, marketing, personnel, physical facilities, and so on – to meet that objective. The extent to which you begin with the end in mind often determines whether or not you are able to create a successful enterprise. Most business failures begin in the first creation, with problems such as undercapitalisation, misunderstanding of the market, or lack of a business plan.

Mapping your time management goal path with an end in mind will give you a sense of direction and allow you to make informed decisions about the best route. As with most journeys, the road to mastering your time may have many twists and potholes. It is important to remember that the route may change but the final destination (mastery of time) will remain the same. There may also be times when you want to give up or the journey has become too difficult. You may even question your decision-making capabilities. If this happens, re-read your goals and pay particular attention to the ER part of your goal. Just like a road trip, take a rest, re-energise yourself, and set off again.

Write down your journey. The route you eventually decide upon will also be influenced by your destination position, your 'end in mind'. On the right-hand side of a piece of A4 paper, write down the characteristics you will display when you are a master of your time. This is where you will end up and shouldn't be confused with part of the journey.

Current position	Best route	Desired position
Slave to the clock	*Solutions*	*Master of your time*

Once you have written your desired position, you need to list the key indicators of your current position. Use the same techniques as before by writing down the reasons why you are a slave to the clock. This list should be on the left-hand side of the paper. It is important to determine all the factors as they will have a significant impact on the route chosen.

The best route is mapped out by eliminating the reasons you are a slave and implementing the techniques, skills and expertise of the

'Victory belongs to the most persevering.'

Napoleon Bonaparte

master. This route will be determined as you progress through the book. Your map is determined by a series of decision-making questions. When such a decision is to be made, ask yourself, 'Will it take me closer to my goal or further away?' If the answer is closer, you are on the right road.

Step 4: Getting started

'You may delay, but time will not.'
Benjamin Franklin

Using the 24-hour 'will do rule' is crucial, as getting started can be a large stumbling block for people. Delay tactics are often used by slaves to the clock. They will seek out 'justifiable' reasons, such as:

> I'm waiting on a reply from someone before I can proceed
> I need to finish this first
> I still have plenty of time before the deadline
> I'm too busy to think about my time management strategy
> It is always better to start at the beginning of a month

Although there are a few different ways to get started, here are some easy-to-use techniques that will help you with your 24-hour 'will do rule':

- Once you have set your goals, always write down your first step
- Make your first step small and easy to complete
- Keep it simple and try not to require the assistance of others as this will lead to possible delays
- Reward yourself as soon as you pass your first milestone

Not knowing where or how to begin can also lead to delays, highlighted by the familiar 'I'll start this tomorrow' comfort phrase. The 'will do rule' is simple: you must complete a task, any task related to achieving your goal, within 24 hours of setting that specific goal.

The reason why the 24-hour rule works is that once you have outlined your goal you are full of excitement, enthusiasm and have a strong wish to achieve it. Your desired position is clear in your mind and you are now at the peak of your motivation curve. The old saying 'strike while the iron is hot' is very apt for this situation. The longer you delay starting, the greater the risk of procrastination.

Step 5: Tell people about your plan

'When everything seems to be going against you, remember that the airplane takes off against the wind, not with it.'
Henry Ford

Publicise your goal: the secret of your success is not to keep it a secret. Tell some trusted friends or work colleagues about your plan and the reasons why you want to master your time. They will give you much-needed support and encouragement if obstacles start to appear. Maybe some of your co-workers are interested in improving their time management skills and you can start a buddy system.

Show your plan to someone who will give you constructive feedback. Explain to them that you would like to give them a weekly progress report and that you value their feedback. This will also instill a level of accountability as there will be someone who will now check up on you.

Step 6: Analyse and make necessary changes

Some people can become very disheartened when their meticulously thought-out plan starts to go off the rails or simply fails. A friend of mine recently told me a great story about her experience at Weight Watchers. Like most people who want to lose weight, she had been talking about doing it for months (in fact years) before she committed to the programme seriously. She had tried a whole host of diets, including every fashionable and celebrity-endorsed one, and had failed gracefully. Once again she stuck rigidly to the diet and exercise regime given to her. The plan was that she would lose a certain amount of weight each week. Week one went according to the plan, week two went a little astray (she had a big celebration party that week) and week three was a disaster as she gained a couple of pounds.

Just as she was about to give up again her trainer explained a life-altering fact to her. He said, 'It has taken you 10 years to build up this excess weight; you can't expect to lose it all in just three weeks unless you want to starve yourself. It takes time. Your plan will get you there, but be patient and persistent. Remember you will need to change your plan as you discover what works and what doesn't work for you personally.' How right he was, because not only did she reach her target weight, but she maintained it.

The same mindset is applicable to becoming a master of your time. It may have taken you a number of years to become enslaved to the clock so these bad habits could take time to be unlearnt while the new improved habits are embedded. Also, what works for your friends or colleagues may not work for you, so ensure your action plan is flexible. Tailor your plan to meet your needs.

The following steps of Audit → Remain flexible → Modify can guide you in evaluating your plan to ensure you achieve your 'best way to use my time' goal.

Audit. 'You can't have a plan and not an audit,' says William G. Kuchta, vice-president of organisational development at Paychex Inc. Once you have started to implement some of the action points in your plan, review their impact. What milestones on your journey to freedom have you accomplished? Have the tasks achieved what they were intended to do? Have the benefits outweighed the cost of the changes you have made? Some of the actions taken may have had unexpected outcomes, both positively and negatively. Analysing your results now will give you

You know you are a slave to the clock when:

- You regularly look at your watch during lunch time
- Meetings run into one another because you attend too many
- You regularly do the work that someone else should be doing
- You worry constantly about deadlines
- Being late is a habit
- Your favourite line has become 'I don't have time to…'
- You bring work home
- You routinely work late
- You have difficulty saying no
- There is a feeling of guilt when you take a break or time off

an opportunity to investigate other options if necessary, which may yield better results. Monitor your progress carefully.

Remain flexible. There is a fine line between being persistent and being pig-headed. An action plan is a flexible, living document and should be reviewed on a regular basis. If your plan is not working, be prepared to seek out alternative solutions. Keeping your plan flexible will also allow you to take advantage of any unexpected opportunities.

Having a flexible plan is not the same as changing the goalposts every time you encounter an obstacle and get a new idea. The end result should remain consistent, but the solutions may change based on any number of factors. Keep your eyes firmly on the finishing line.

Modify. If something isn't working you don't necessarily have to change your entire plan. By modifying it you could develop a better or different solution. A key point to remember is that your plan is made up of a range of solutions, which will get you to your goal. Top performers aren't afraid to try out new ideas to develop more productive habits that will help them achieve their goals. They will attempt different approaches and then evaluate their effectiveness. This builds their persistence. Thomas A. Edison said, 'Just because something doesn't do what you planned it to do doesn't mean it's useless.'

How to spot a slave to the clock

People often become slaves to the clock without realising it. They never set out to intentionally become a slave but the clock somehow crept up on them and trapped them. It started to gain control gradually over a period of time. These people display classic signs of clock domination that they fail to recognise and acknowledge. They run from one meeting to the next without being fully briefed and usually are a few minutes late. They schedule appointment after appointment, filling their calendar, which leaves very little time for preparations or over-runs. As for deadlines, they are seen as a challenge or movable target, rather than a completion date.

These slave-like behaviours are often easier to spot in other people than to recognise in yourself. As a result, there are many people suffering the effects of such behaviour who are unable to break free.

Take a risk

To become a master of your time, you need to focus like a top athlete and have the right mindset. You need discipline, a real desire for success and to take responsibility for your performance. Billie Jean King, one of the greatest tennis players of all time, said, 'Champions take responsibility. When the ball is coming over the net, you can be sure I want the ball.' Having an anything-is-possible attitude greatly enhances your chances of being a true master of your time.

A creative and brilliant imagination will seek out opportunities to improve how you manage yourself and those around you, which will bring the biggest rewards. Creativity is often suppressed by people's bosses, who would rather work by the 'we always do it this way' principle, or by well-meaning family and friends who unfortunately have limited vision and therefore live by the 'don't dream too big or you might have a big fall' principle. Mastering how you use your time will often involve some element of risk as you break free from your comfort zone.

Bill Gates, in his article about the Wright Brothers in *Time* magazine, spoke about the importance of vision, perseverance and creativity, without which the Wright Brothers would not have discovered arguably the most important invention of the 20th century, the aeroplane. Gates wrote,

> Wilbur and Orville Wright were two brothers from the heartland of America with a vision as sweeping as the sky and a practicality as down-to-earth as the Wright Cycle Co., the bicycle business they founded in Dayton, Ohio, in 1892. But while there were countless bicycle shops in turn-of-the-century America, in only one were wings being built as well as wheels. When the Wright brothers finally realized their vision of powered human flight in 1903, they made the world a forever smaller place. I've been to Kitty Hawk, North Carolina, and seen where the brothers imagined the future, and then literally flew across its high frontier. It was an inspiration to be there, and to soak up the amazing perseverance and creativity of these two pioneers.

Some of the tools and techniques discussed in this book will work for you while others won't. You need to personalise this entire book and work your plan like a real champion, a real visionary. Ask and answer the hard questions posed to see if you are a slave to the clock or master of your time. Take the tools, even if you tried them before, and look at how you can use them to bring your vision into your world. Take control and responsibility for your time. Don't be discouraged by other people just because it didn't work for them. Persistence and dedication to excellence will bring improvement.

You know you are a master of your time when:

- Your workload increases but you still manage to leave work on time
- You get the right jobs done first
- You continually seek improvement and innovation in how you use your time
- You can delegate effectively
- You only attend productive meetings
- You have a clutter-free working environment
- You can take a break without feeling guilty
- You avoid time-stealers with ruthless determination
- You manage yourself and those around you and let time take care of itself

INTRODUCING MASTER OF TIME TO THE HOME

This weekend, how much time did you spend doing the things that
mean something to you? How much time did you spend with your
loved ones? On Sunday night, did you reflect on your weekend and feel
that you got real value for the way you spent your weekend? Did you
have any regrets? Are you facing Monday refreshed and energised?

'Live every day as if it were the last' is a line in a poem that sums
up the philosophy that masters of time live up to. Their lives are not a
collection of ifs, buts or maybes. They are not disillusioned with their lot
because they are in control of how they use their time. They have developed good habits that work for them. Their home life is built around
the activities that bring happiness, enjoyment and are value-driven.

Mary Kennedy wrote a book of quotes and poems that both her mother
and herself found inspiring. *Lines I Love* is a book full of hope and passion
for life. It is also a reminder that life can be full of challenges and regret,
as so eloquently demonstrated by English dramatist James Albery's epi-
taph, which also illustrates why it is so easy to be a slave to the clock:

> He slept beneath the moon,
> He basked beneath the sun,
> He lived a life of going to do,
> And died with nothing done!

Masters of time live the life they want to live, doing the things that
bring value to them. There is no room for wasteful activities in their
daily routines. They are full of enthusiasm, optimism and energy, with
a knack of turning dreams into reality. Charity work, helping out with
the children's sport clubs, learning a new skill or language, exercising
regularly and indulging in lifelong hobbies are a regular feature of their
day. They always seem to have enough time to do the really important
things in life.

There are no regrets in their world because they believe in using
their time wisely. 'Fairytale of New York' is a classic tale sung soulfully by
Shane McGowan and Kirsty MacColl, in which they sing those immortal
words, 'I could have been someone, well so could anyone.' Everyone can
be a master of time if they really want to be; all they need is passion and
commitment. Equally, everyone can be slaves to the clock, and most
aren't even aware of their condition. It is your decision – invest in your
skills, knowledge and self-management, and reap the benefits.

What's interesting about you?

Have you ever been asked to talk about your hobbies or an interesting fact about yourself, and all that you could muster up was some vague, clichéd activities, like reading and walking? In fact, the most interesting facts about you were the things that you would love to do but still hadn't found the time to. You had a fabulous range of 'I wish I had the time to do them' hobbies. It is now time to stop thinking about these important activities and start living them.

Develop a vision for your life by using the same skills you have used in your working environment. Always start with a clear understanding of the end result. Articulate your dreams by simply writing them down on a page. Include how you will feel when you are spending your time the way you want to. Then ask yourself a few simple questions to establish how you will get there. Suddenly the barriers that were preventing you from living your life the way you wanted to live it are no longer insurmountable. Set SMARTER goals to help you build the focus that you need to turn your vision into your way of life.

Once you have written your blueprint for success, then make a commitment to yourself to complete these goals so that you can enjoy the benefits straight away. Don't waste any more time blaming the clock. It is not the lack of time that is stopping you, it is you. Tell someone close to you about your new commitments. This in turn will become a set of new habits, which you will allocate time to completing.

Before you read any further, take a break and write down the first part of your plan.

Dos and don'ts of managing time

Do: Be a master
- Understand you cannot manage time, you must manage yourself and those around you and let time take care of itself
- Have a plan
- Set SMARTER time goals
- Be decisive
- Modify as necessary your journey to freedom
- Begin with a vision in mind

Don't: Be a slave
- Blame others for your poor use of time
- Give up when you encounter an obstacle
- Never have enough time for the things that are important to you

PERSONAL THOUGHTS

What will I do differently tomorrow?

MYTH NO. 2
TO-DO LISTS ARE THE ANSWER TO MY TIME MANAGEMENT WOES

IT'S NOT THAT SIMPLE

After attending the obligatory time management course to improve his chances of meeting his numerous report deadlines, John returned to work full of confidence and enthusiasm. He marched to his desk, head held high, armed with this life-changing tool he wholeheartedly believed would transform the way he worked. His job would never be the same again – no more stress; failed deadlines would be a thing of the past; and his boss would put him forward for the next promotion. Or so he thought.

The answer to his time management problems was so simple, he was embarrassed he hadn't thought of it himself. Mastering this fantastic tool would ensure that John was no longer a slave to deadlines and clock-watching. It would ensure that he was no longer overwhelmed by ever-increasing workloads. He would never, ever forget to do an important task again. Alex, his demanding and less-than-trusting boss, would no longer have to chase him for outstanding work, and he would become the most organised and efficient worker in the company. John's new best friend was the all conquering to-do list.

Long before anyone else had arrived at the office, John, with renewed optimism, sat down at his rather messy and cluttered desk where he somehow found a new A4 notepad. He immediately started to compile the list of tasks he would complete that day. Although at the training course he had been offered (among a host of other time-saving devices)

'Unless commitment is made, there are only promises and hopes... but no plans'.

Peter F. Drucker

23

an online to-do list toolkit from his new time management guru and mentor, John opted for the simple pen-and-paper version. He was convinced the to-do list would be his saviour. No more embarrassing admissions of failure or the dreaded schoolboy march to his boss's office, no more late-night, frantic endeavouring to complete those dreaded monthly reports.

Twenty minutes passed and John was still writing down all the tasks he needed to complete. Some were routine jobs, while others were large, complicated assignments. He remembered that at the course it was advised that large tasks should be broken down into smaller, more manageable tasks. This process was taking longer than he expected. Undeterred, he pressed on and finally he finished his to-do list. There were 53 items on the list and it took approximately 35 minutes to complete. Was this the best use of his time, he wondered?

Slightly dispirited that the to-do list took so long to prepare and that there were so many items on it, John reassured himself that this was the way forward as he was now planning his day. That old cliché, 'Failure to plan is planning to fail,' sprang to mind, and he was determined his name would no longer be associated with missed deadlines. He felt organised, in control and excited about crossing items off the list as he completed them.

As the day drew to a close, John took some time out after returning from his third meeting to review his to-do list. He had managed to cross off 11 items as fully completed and he had started three other items. Unfortunately, as a result of the meetings he had added a further eight items to the list during the day. Crucially, he had missed another deadline as he hadn't factored in the length of time the meetings would eat up. This was not the outcome he'd been promised at the time management course or had been expecting.

The next day, despite the frustration of seeing the to-do list fail on its maiden voyage, John decided to give it another chance to see if it would improve his performance. He started the process again by listing all the tasks he didn't complete the day before, and then he listed the new day's tasks. Not surprisingly things didn't improve on day two. It was all so simple on the training course: the theory was plan your day and stick to your plan. This was easier said than done as colleagues, customers and a demanding boss all conspired to guarantee that John's best laid plans went awry before he could even start. Robert Burns wrote in his poem 'To a Mouse, On Turning Her Up in her Nest with the Plough':

But Mouse, you are not alone,
In proving foresight may be vain:
The best laid schemes of mice and men
Go often askew,
And leave us nothing but grief and pain,
For promised joy!

As the theory and reality collided in John's world there was a sudden realisation that to-do lists on their own wouldn't be his saviour. By the end of the week he had given up on the to-do lists because all he was doing was changing the date at the top of the paper since most of the list was still outstanding. The to-do lists had become the not-done or likely-to-be-done-today list. John was totally demoralised.

Obsessed with lists

Many people, just like John, return from a time management training course or read a time management book and are convinced that merely writing a list of tasks to be completed will in some way transform their performance level. They are convinced that a to-do list will radically change how they manage their time. They will then spend endless hours writing lists for everything, in the fool-hardy notion that this will somehow make them more efficient. Making lists has almost become a national past-time. Katherine Rosman wrote in the *Wall Street Journal* that there is a 'growing appetite for list making' and that a lot of companies are producing products to feed this 21st-Century planning principle.

There are now to-do lists for every major event in your life. Things you should do before you die, books you must read, films you must see and places you must visit. Then there are the helpful to-do lists: jobs you want to do before going on holidays, items to buy for your holidays, and the ultimate to-do list, which is things to do to ensure you enjoy your holiday. These humble lists can also be very revealing. According to Sasha Cagen, author of *To-Do List: From Buying Milk to Finding a Soul Mate, What Our Lists Reveal About Us*, to-do lists can reflect your idiosyncrasies, personalities and passions.

Technology is also playing its part in pushing the notion that to-do lists can solve your time management problems. Innovative technology is constantly changing the features and usability of the to-do list, which is either improving things or making them more complex, depending on your point of view. There are many websites offering you online versions of to-do lists. *USA Today* featured Ta-da Lists as one of its Hot Sites. This is a free Web-based tool, which boasts over 4 million lists have been downloaded. The to-do lists you can use include what to do on holidays, what to pack for the holiday and what presents to buy while on holidays. In fact, you could plan your entire trip by using the various to-do lists.

People have become slaves to their lists. They have become obsessed with writing them and endeavouring to complete them. Most set themselves up for failure by writing a list of things they will never be able to complete. They focus on writing the list instead of the principle behind writing it. No wonder to-do lists fail for so many people.

Understanding the principle behind to-do lists

Padraig Harrington, winner of the British Open in 2007, always lists what he wants to achieve at the start of every golf season. He knows that this will drive him on to greater success each year, otherwise complacency could set in. His list is not just a list of things to do. He carefully outlines what he needs to do in order to achieve his targets. He plans for success with the same dedication and precision he displays in his game. He doesn't share these lists with the general public as he believes that to-do lists could be used negatively; they could become judgmental rather than motivational. He declares in *Journey to the Open* that

> winning The Open has been a personal dream. However, I must now set clear goals for myself to keep my focus going forward… but I can say that I now want to build on this success and become the best player I possibly can.

To-do lists should be your map to success and not just a list of things you might do or would like to do. The main principle behind these lists is that they clear your mind of unnecessary clutter because you have now written it down. You can see clearly what you want to achieve and therefore you can focus your energy on achieving it.

Is your to-do list working for you?

It is now commonplace for workers to spend too much time fire-fighting urgent requests and not enough time planning. They react to the demands of their job and focus on getting things done rather than managing their job. Like a wheel caught in soft sand, they work very hard but never seem to move forward. The ability to plan is an important managerial function according to Henri Fayol, who was a key figure in the Classical School of Management. He believed that, to be effective and efficient, it is necessary for managers to decide what tasks need to be completed, devise a plan of action and then implement this plan. This process introduces order and control. To become a true master of your time, you must master the art of planning and forecasting.

However, there is a need to get the balance right between planning what to do and actually doing it. Peters and Waterman (*In Search of Excellence*, 1982) concluded that one of the attributes of successful companies was a 'bias for action'. There is a need to get on with the process of completing tasks: over-planning or over-analysing can restrict progress and therefore success. Take action on your to-do list (your plan) as quickly as possible and then analyse the result of this action; make any necessary changes and proceed to the next step of your plan.

Not surprisingly, to-do lists have, in recent times, received some bad press initiated by disgruntled workers who have become disillusioned by increased workloads and the inability of the to-do list to help them cope. People rashly discard the lists as they unfairly blame them for failing rather than examining why this tool failed them. They complain that the lists take too long to compose and that as soon as you have completed your plan for the day, you get a call from your boss or customer. This usually results in the plan being thrown out the window because their request has now suddenly become a top priority. Everything else is put to one side.

These are just excuses made by people who have allowed their lists to enslave them because they have failed to use this tool properly. They have overstated the importance and capabilities of the to-do list, resulting in the inevitable sense of being let down. Unable to see the real purpose and benefit of their list through the haze of their frustrations, they simply give up. They don't take the time to unearth the real reason why their to-do list was unsuccessful for them.

Why do to-do lists fail?

To-do lists fail for a variety of reasons. They are usually written in a way that promotes failure. Instead of being a helpful aid to completing more tasks during the day, they are more likely to be the dreaded list of what you didn't achieve. They are mostly a negative tool for people as they are a random list of tasks that need to be completed with no connection to the time available. People make lists without considering time. The main reasons why to-do lists fail are:

- They take to too long to compose
- There are too many items on the list
- There isn't enough time to complete everything on the list
- People fail to prioritise the items on the list
- People spend too much time planning and not enough time doing
- The list becomes the procrastination list
- The list is overwhelming
- The fear of deadlines
- The lists have become overcomplicated
- The lists are thrown away at the end of each day

In the reasons listed above a common theme surfaces. The lists fail not because of the principle behind the to-do list; they fail because people are unable or unwilling to manage themselves and those around them. They allow procrastination to dictate what doesn't get done; they prefer the comfort of planning rather than doing because it is safer, and they are easily discouraged by the volume of tasks to be completed. The reason why to-do lists aren't as successful as they should be is that people fail to manage themselves effectively.

Back to basics

Traditionally, a to-do list was seen as a simple but efficient way to plan your day. It involved determining what your key tasks were and their priority level. You then worked your way through this list, starting with the top priority tasks and ticking them off when completed. This gave people a sense of satisfaction as they worked their way down their daily list. An additional benefit to using to-do lists was that people would also have a record of what they had achieved that day.

The many tips given about writing to-do lists talk about starting with a master list, which is a list of all the things you want to do. This is usually quite a long list. Then it is suggested that from this list you write your daily to-do list, which is much shorter. It is recommended by the experts that this job should be completed at the end of the day so that you can have a clear run when you arrive at work the next day. These lists are then reviewed weekly to measure your progress. Another tip is that you should delegate any task that isn't important and that you ruthlessly work your way through your list.

To fully benefit from to-do lists it is now time to develop this principle further and make it work for you. A winning recipe for the successful use of to-do lists is to keep the composition of the list simple, the strategy for completion focused and the outcomes monitored.

'Simplicity is the ultimate sophistication.'

Leonardo da Vinci

A to-do list is only as good as what is written in it

Mastering the art of writing to-do lists requires some basic writing skills. In their book *This Business of Writing*, authors Terry Prone and Kieran Lyons tell us, 'Good professional writing always starts with [Rudyard] Kipling's "six serving-men": What, Why, When, How, Where and Who, in no particular order.' The principle of good writing is as applicable to writing a to-do list as it is to any other form of writing. They continue, 'Don't kid yourself that talking about what you're writing is the same as writing. It isn't.' You can talk all day about what you are going to do, but until you commit these tasks to paper they will remain thoughts and not actions. Writing to-do lists is your blueprint to successfully completing the tasks that are of real value to you.

To-do lists often fail because people write what they have to do on their lists and forget the why, where, how, what, when and who. They forget that the strategy for achieving what's on the to-do list is equally or even more important than what is on the list. The list tells you what you already know – why, where, how, what, when and who will guide you to the successful completion of your list. Here's how you can apply Kipling's 'six serving-men' to writing a to-do list.

Why do I need a to-do list?

Before you waste any more time writing another to-do list that doesn't work for you, ask yourself the critical question: Why am I writing this list? The answer to this question will help you to focus on the real purpose behind your need to plan your day. This should become the main driving force behind the success of your lists.

As a result of some soul-searching, you may conclude there is a need to rebrand the humble to-do list as one of the problems with these lists is that they have become nagging lists. They are a list of things you have to do rather than what you want to do. They stare at you from yellow Post-its plastered around your PC screen, from the fridge door, from the wall or divider surrounding your work area. They are everywhere, reminding you of what you haven't done or are likely to do. They are really lists of tasks you are trying to forget to do or wish someone else would do for you. People are enslaved and demoralised by their lists.

It is now time to rebrand your to-do lists and make them 'I really want to complete these tasks lists'. A compelling case for a name change is that the name should reflect the primary function of your to-do list. It should spell out what it does for you in a clear and concise manner. It needs to be positive and reassure you that what it promises, it can deliver. Pick a name that will personalise your to-do list for you. Some people now call their to-do lists their 'I will complete today list', 'my champion checklist', 'my success list'. Whatever name you choose, ensure that the name is results driven, positive, and reflects your desire to be a master of your time.

In this book the to-do list will be rebranded and called the adding-value list, as every task on the list should add value in some way to you, your boss or your organisation. Adding-value lists will focus you on achieving worthwhile results, results that are important. Masters of time have a habit of doing the things that slaves to the clock fail to do. They identify what tasks add real value and then complete them, even when they are reluctant to do so. Slaves to the clock will always find an excuse not to complete these tasks. Using adding-value lists will encourage you to direct your energy to completing high-priority tasks and dumping the low-value tasks. It will help you to develop a ruthless attitude to only doing the things that really matter to you. It requires hard work and diligence as it is easy to fall back into old habits of listing all the things you need to do and ending up doing very little.

Rebranding the to-do list is not just a name change. It is about revitalising and repositioning to-do lists in your performance and time management strategy. It requires a change of mindset. It is about thinking about the real purpose of to-do lists and how they can help you to become a master of your time. Your to-do list needs energy, focus and an ability to deliver on its promise.

Your adding-value lists are more than a mere list of tasks. They are an essential component of your new time management strategy, which is managing yourself to manage others. They produce an instant snapshot of where you are at any given moment: what tasks you are currently working on, their priority level, what capacity you have and how effective and efficient your performance levels are. Your adding-value list is your carefully thought-out plan for success. It will also assist you in managing your manager and controlling the flow of additional work in your direction.

Where should you keep your 'adding-value list'?

Now that you understand the importance of answering the *why* question, you can proceed to examine where you should keep your adding-value list. John, like many people, wrote his to-do list on a writing pad. He had thought about using one of the many electronic options available but decided on this, the simple and flexible pen-and-paper method. It suited his needs. Whether you choose high-tech sophistication or simplicity, it is often the location of your adding-value list and not your method that will determine how successful your lists are. For John, the lack of thought given to where he should locate his adding-value list proved to be his undoing.

Imagine making an important financial decision such as applying for a loan to buy a car or a new home and basing your decision on only part of the information available to you. You look at the monthly repayments the loan will require and decide you can afford it because your monthly income is greater than the monthly repayment. Unfortunately, you omit to factor in all the additional monthly outgoings you currently undertake. However, you still commit to the loan and go ahead and purchase the car or house. Does this make good financial sense? Clearly, it doesn't, and that is why lenders carry out a full financial assessment to establish if you can really afford the monthly repayment. They look at all your outgoings and compile an affordability study of your financial affairs. This full assessment also takes into consideration whether you could still afford the loan if the monthly payments were to increase. This is a prudent and sensible approach to important financial decisions. The same approach should be taken with adding-value lists.

Whilst adding-value lists are easy to compose, they will not be successful if viewed in isolation. They form only part of what you do on any given day. Most people have a traditional to-do list and a separate business appointment diary. All scheduling devices (diaries, holiday planners, etc.) should be integrated into one system. The best and easiest system to use is your diary (paper or electronic), as it has a record of all of your appointments, holidays, meetings and any other activity you must perform as part of your duties.

Locating your adding-value lists in your diary will ensure that you have a full and complete picture of all of your daily activities. It will improve your decision-making process as it will allow you to make better assessments about the length of time a task will take, as well as its start time, since you will now have all the relevant information stored in one

It is important to remember that to-do lists are not:

- Shopping lists of the things you would like to do
- A list of tasks you have no chance of completing
- An unstructured list of tasks
- A weapon of demotivation
- A nagging list
- A rigid lists of tasks

location. Using your adding-value lists to plan your tasks can only be successful if they are developed with complete and accurate information.

How to structure your adding-value lists

The first step to building a successful adding-value list is to divide the page of your diary into five columns. Each column should contain the following headings:

Brief description of task	Adding-value reason	Estimated length of time	Actual time	Priority level

Then write down the entire list of your adding-value tasks for the day. Although some of these tasks may be things you must complete every day, it is still essential to write them down as it will help you to build a complete picture of the day. This will consolidate all your tasks into one place. You should also include all of the activities you would normally put into your diary, such as meetings, appointments, holidays (yours and key colleagues') and corporate functions.

Once you have completed your daily list, progress to the first draft of your weekly and monthly schedule for your adding-value list. This schedule will give you a snapshot of your work, which will help you monitor your capacity for additional tasks. It will identify any potential work overload problems, when tasks should realistically start, and work-flow patterns. It also helps to move you from a daily fire-fighting mindset to a more strategic focus.

You should plan your following day's activities before you leave the office. This is effective because it avoids potential distractions at the start of the day. By identifying a simple task to get on with first thing in the morning, you will create a positive environment at the start of your day that will give you the incentive to continue in the same way.

Adding-value lists are fundamentally important for efficient working habits. Using them each day will help you to remember all your key tasks while reducing stress levels. They will also improve how you use your time. Most of all, as you will see in the next stage, it will help you prioritise your work flow.

What tasks should be on an adding-value list?

The simple rule of thumb is that the only tasks that should be on your adding-value list are the ones that will add real value to you, your boss, your colleagues, your customers or your organisation. That is not saying you shouldn't do other non-value tasks; sometimes these tasks have to be completed. Standing around having a chat about last night's latest TV 'water-cooler moment' or doing some shredding may not add any great value to anyone but sometimes these things are unavoidable. However, they shouldn't be on your list of things that need to be done. Spontaneous wasting of time or doing a non-value task isn't wrong; it's how often and when you allow it to happen, or putting it on a to-do list that causes the problems.

Reason why the task is on your list. Identifying the reason why a task is on your adding-value list is a good way of keeping your list concise and workable. In your diary you have divided your adding-value lists section into five columns. In the first column you should write down each adding-value task you will work on that day. A brief description of the task is useful; it helps to paint the overall picture of the day. In the next column write down the reason why you need to complete this task. Who will benefit from this task? Keep the reason clear and concise. This will help you when you start to prioritise your list.

Once you have completed the second column, reread the reasons why each task is on your list. You must now decide if these reasons add value or not. If not, then that task should be omitted from your adding-value list. Although these tasks need to be done, you need to develop a different strategy for dealing with them. Try delegating them to someone more junior than you, or to someone who has more time available.

The first time you undertake this exercise, you should also try to establish if you are completing certain tasks out of habit. Ask yourself a simple question: 'Is this the most important task that I can be doing at this moment in time?' If the answer if no, then you should consider dumping the task for something more important.

When should I do each task?

The next key component required to build successful adding-value lists is your ability to budget and plan. Knowing how much time each task will realistically take and when the most productive time of your day is will yield the best results. Understanding Italian economist Vilfredo

Pareto's 80/20 rule can play a pivotal role in achieving outstanding results. He created a mathematical formula in 1906 to explain what he had observed about the wealth of his country, which was that in Italy 80 per cent of income went to 20 per cent of the people. Further theorists, including Joseph M. Juran, suggested that Pareto's Principle could be applied to many aspects of business management. For instance, 80 per cent of sales are generated through 20 per cent of your customer base. Therefore it is vital that you know which customers fall into the 20 per cent range. If you apply Pareto's Principle to your adding-value lists, then completing 80 per cent of your adding-value tasks will only take 20 per cent of your time. Masters of their time will always ensure that they protect this 20 per cent of their day to ensure outstanding results from their adding-value lists.

In the third column, assign each of your adding-value tasks a start time and an estimated finish time. You must be realistic when you allocate the time to each task. When describing a property, real-estate agents will paint a picture of how close the property is to important amenities or to a major shopping centre. They will write such statements as, 'This property is 20 minutes from the bustling city centre.' This may be factually correct at 6:30 on a Sunday morning when you are driving a Ferrari; however, in rush-hour traffic, the journey time could be nearer to 60 minutes.

The same principle applies to budgeting your time on your adding-value list. If a task takes 20 minutes to complete when there are no interruptions and you have all the necessary items to complete it, then schedule it for a time of the day when you will not be interrupted, your protected time. If this is not possible, then you must factor the expected interruptions you will encounter into your budget. You must be realistic with your time budget, otherwise you will not have a true and complete picture of your day.

Finally, in the last column, write down the actual time the task took to complete. Also write down the reason for any discrepancy between the last two columns as this should help you the next time you need to complete the task. Use this column as your learning tool and build yourself a personal management information system. Developing an in-depth understanding of your work patterns will help you plan your day in the most productive and satisfying way.

Who: **Concentrate on results, not being busy**

Who you are completing the tasks for on your adding-value lists needs to be addressed; this will form the basis of getting the right jobs done first. Prioritising your list is about making choices between what to do and what not to do as well as when to do it. To prioritise effectively you need to be able to recognise the tasks that are important, as well as to understand the difference between urgent and important. The other question that needs to be answered is, who are the tasks important to? In reality all tasks are important to someone; you need to understand which tasks are important to you and your key stakeholders.

Once you have completed writing down the enire list of tasks on your adding-value list, you can start to organise them according to the importance and urgency of each task. This can be sorted in the last column. You can classify your adding-value lists by using the grid below as follows:

A. Urgent and important – work on it now
B. Urgent but not important – work on it if you have time or else delegate
C. Important but not urgent – start it today before it becomes urgent
D. Not important and not urgent – dump it if possible

Priority grid

A Work on it now	**B** Work on it if you have time or else delegate
C Start it today before it becomes urgent	**D** Dump it if possible

Who should be top priority on your 'adding-value list'? Understanding the difference between 'urgent' and 'urgent and important' is paramount if you are to prioritise effectively. The other important ingredient is deciding on who you are prioritising your tasks for as this will determine who should get their requests completed first. This decision should not be based on who shouts the loudest or who causes you the most grief – the decision should be based on which tasks add the most value to you.

Master your time

Prioritise your list of tasks for today.

Understanding your audience will help you when it comes to prioritising your adding-value lists. Your focus should always be on the important tasks. Work on the tasks that are important to your key stakeholders. Manage yourself like a business and identify the tasks that will give you the best return on your time.

Busy doing the right things or busy doing the wrong things?

Nowadays everyone is busy doing things. They are rushing around endeavouring to beat the clock. Tight deadlines and excessive workloads are fuelling this busyness culture. It is sometimes frowned upon not to be busy; in fact some people will act busy in order to be seen in a positive light. Organisations often equate being busy with being productive. However, whereas it is true that most people are truly busy in today's working environment, many are busy doing the wrong tasks.

Developing the skill of prioritising will allow you to consistently work on important tasks as a priority. Instead of constantly fire-fighting with urgent tasks you should be spending at least 20 per cent of your time working on important, but not urgent, tasks. This represents 1.5 hours per day and it will keep you strategically focused on the key tasks. Applying Pareto's Principle means that you will achieve 80 per cent of your key value-added tasks during this protected 1.5 hours.

How to use the priority grid

Learning how to use the priority grid is not the same as knowing how to prioritise. Scheduling your adding-value list is easy once you have learnt a few basic principles. Putting it into practice requires strong managerial skills.

Masters of time have the ability to protect their Green Priority C time. Every day they work on important but not urgent tasks. These are tasks that can be easily postponed as they are not urgent. No one but you will know whether you have put in the effort to get them done. True masters believe that every hour spent in Green Priority C time is time well spent. This ability to forward-plan means that they spend less time fire-fighting in the Red Priority A space. They realise that the more time and energy they spend in the Green Zone means that there are less tasks falling into the stressful Red Zone.

A slave to the clock, on the other hand, will spend more of their time in the dreaded B and D Zones and, as a consequence, the tasks build up in the Red Zone A. They are unable to see a way of breaking this cycle and will continue to fire-fight Red Zone A tasks. They will blame everything and everyone for their blight. Slaves to the clock are prone to be reactive, rather than proactive. They lack the imagination to build a working environment that promotes a culture of planning and forward-thinking. They believe they are controlled by their work, rather than being able to control their work.

Energy levels

Have you ever noticed that there are parts of the day when you get more tasks completed than at other times? Your energy levels are higher and you just seem to complete tasks effortlessly. The job is fun and rewarding. Then there are the periods during the day when you tend to daydream a lot or sit there thinking about what to do. Your energy levels are low and every task takes longer to complete. You are easily distracted and are prone to lose interest in the task at hand.

Identify your energy levels and work patterns as this will boost your productivity. If you can align your high energy time with your pro-tected Green Zone C time then you will reach peak performance levels. In low-energy periods, focus on Grey Zone D tasks, such as filing and returning calls to friends and colleagues. These activities won't require too much attention.

There are many suggested ways to improve your drive at work, including regular exercise, better diet, napping and yoga. Anne McGee-Cooper suggests in her book *You Don't Have to Go Home from Work Exhausted!* that

> there are many way to restore energy during the day and the night, and sleeping is just one of them. Time spent exercising, playing, laughing, having fun, being creative, relaxing, meditating, and switching to other activities can also renew your momentum and increase your alertness. And you can do these energy-building activities throughout the day rather than wait for bedtime to restore your energy.

Include in your adding-value list time for recharging the batteries – this is not a time-wasting activity. It is a crucial investment in main-taining high energy levels when they are required most. Get creative during your lunch and resist the temptation to sit around and partake in a negative moaning session with your colleagues. Get out there and revitalise yourself. Fifteen or twenty minutes of positive activities during your lunch will have a big effect on your performance in the afternoon.

Top performers 'need to know their own productivity patterns. Some stars are most productive when they give their all in a defined burst of intense activity. They go at their work like a crazed person, often working fourteen-hour workdays until the project is done. Once the project is completed, they will need a lot of down time before they can work back up to that intensity again. Others stars schedule their projects with a steady rhythm, moving easily from one to the next.'

Robert E. Kelly

Work in progress

Building successful adding-value lists is the blueprint for taking control of your work and your performance. They are designed to ensure that you achieve your personal goals as outlined in your vision statement. This requires a determination to succeed because there are many barriers that can derail you. Your lists will constantly evolve as you and your job develop, but they will bring you great results, results you could only dream about without them. As Padraig Harrington said:

> Part of me feels that everything is possible because from a very young age I always felt that I had the ability, patience and stamina to figure things out. And that, I think, is my real talent – a capacity to work my way through a problem while never losing sight of the goal, and to find the information to keep developing. I've always said that I am a work in progress.

Your adding-value lists are a work in progress that can propel you to great heights. As you complete each task, you move a step closer to achieving your vision.

INTRODUCING MASTER OF TIME TO THE HOME

Prioritise your home schedule

When you arrive home exhausted and stressed after a busy day being a slave to the clock, you often bring with you a huge amount of baggage. The familiar what-went-wrong-today stories: my boss doesn't understand the pressure I'm under; the supplier let me down; the computer crashed; and the 'I'm sad' list goes on. Unfortunately most people forget to bring home the one valuable piece of baggage they have developed during the day, and that is how to be a master of time.

A note of caution, however: writing to-do lists at home can very quickly descend into nagging lists that are left for your partner, children or friends to complete. They can become a list of orders, such as to do the cleaning, shopping, or fixing any number of household items. They are seldom motivational and inspiring.

In this chapter you have developed adding-value lists, which is your strategy to survive in a busy workplace by prioritising your schedule and working with your list rather than being controlled by it. This is based on the principles of:

- Planning and organising
- Knowing what is important
- Managing yourself

Now it is time to bring these winning principles into your home. Develop an adding-value list for your home life. This will help you to have more fun, more hobbies, more energy, more excitement and more time with the people you love and care about. Using an adding-value list will change your life and the lives of those around you.

New lease on life

Developing a positive adding-value list is a conscious decision, which will invigorate you and fill you with positive thoughts and actions. You will deliberately choose activities that bring a sense of meaning to your life. You can create the life you want by simply deciding in advance what you want to do each day. Your home is your sanctuary, so you must concentrate on doing activities that bring you joy and happiness. It a place to recharge your batteries and to spend quality time with the people who are special to you. It is the most important place in your life – it is the place where you truly want to be.

What are you waiting for?

There will never be the perfect time to do all the things you want to do in life. Instead of waiting for that 'right moment in your life', start to live your life now. Move from being reactive to being proactive. Take control by spending just 10 minutes a day deciding on what you are going to do every day that will bring you happiness and fulfilment. It is your responsibility to live your life.

Your personal adding-value list can contain activities that don't take up too much of your time, but because of your busy lifestyle you have got out of the habit of doing them. They could be simple activities, such as phoning friends, listening to great music or simply watching nature breathe new life into your neighbourhood.

Before you read any further, take a break and write down the next part of your plan.

Dos and don'ts of to-do lists

Do: Be a master

- Take action daily on important, long-term projects to ensure their completion before they become time-sensitive
- Understand the difference between urgent and important
- Accomplish more with less stress
- Plan your success
- Focus your energy on what is important to you
- Apply Pareto's Principle to your important but not urgent tasks
- Protect your Green Zone
- Be busy doing the right things
- Rebrand your to-do lists

Don't: Be a slave

- Be busy doing lots of things but unable to make any significant progress on the important tasks
- Become overwhelmed by your to-do list
- Write endless lists with no consideration for the 'how'
- Procrastinate on the important tasks as you spend too much time fire-fighting
- Be unable to plan
- See planning as someone else's responsibility
- Spend too much doing unimportant tasks
- Write to-do lists with no time budgets

PERSONAL THOUGHTS

What will I do differently tomorrow?

MYTH NO. 3
I KNOW HOW I SPEND MY TIME

TIME AUDIT: PRINCIPLES OF EFFECTIVE CONTROL

John started to read an article about a survey carried out by Salary.com, which found that employees on average wasted 2.1 hours per working day. He was perplexed by this statistic. How could anyone waste 2.1 hours in a working day? Nobody in his department could afford to waste so much time. How did they get away with being so inefficient? Was no one managing them? As he looked at his workload piling up on his desk he convinced himself he certainly couldn't waste so much time. Maybe those cocky sales guys could or that shower in marketing. John didn't have much time for them – he felt they were more interested in talking and socialising with colleagues than working.

John decided to continue reading the article as he was fascinated by its findings. He made a cup of coffee and eased himself back into his chair. Although he was very busy, he was easily distracted by what he was reading. The survey found that younger people were more likely to engage in time-wasting activities. He agreed as he felt the younger staff in his department were flighty and didn't show the same commitment as he did. The report also answered the question, 'What are the biggest distractions in the workplace?' It found that surfing the Internet, socialising with co-workers and taking extended or excessive breaks were the biggest offenders. Again John agreed.

The survey results started to annoy John. He could see his colleagues were typical of the people who were so easily distracted. He turned to Rachel, who was in the middle of compiling this week's sales

'Regret for wasted time is more wasted time.'

Mason Cooley

When was the last time you did this?

Carry out a detailed time audit on yourself to discover how you actually spend your time as opposed to how you think you spend your time.

figures for the management committee, and started his rant.

'I told you this place was full of time-wasters and that we're the only ones who do any work around here. No wonder I have so much work on my desk and I never get out of this place at a reasonable time. If the others didn't spend two hours a day gossiping and surfing the Net, maybe we'd get some work done. Read this report – it sums this place up perfectly. It's a holiday camp.'

Rachel read the article and smiled. She knew that John was in this category of time-wasting also, but wouldn't admit to it. He was a news junkie and spent a good part of his morning reading the various news sites online. He saw this activity as research. Most days, however, a news piece would hit a nerve and set John off on one of his crusades.

'Look, Rachel, that's how much time they admit to wasting, I bet it's a lot more if the truth be known. They need tighter management control.'

'I know, John,' she said to humour him, 'but I have to finish the figures so I'll talk to you later. Have you got this week's figures done yet? I need them urgently.'

John, ignoring this request, then turned to Craig and continued his tirade. This went on for a further 20 minutes.

Do you really know how you spend your time?

One of the most precious assets in your life is time. It's free and you don't have to do anything to get it. As a result, most people don't think too much about time or how they spend it. They usually complain that there isn't enough of it and that if they had more of it they would do lots more activities. The lack of time is their favourite excuse for not doing activities like looking after their health, spending more time with their family and friends, and career development. Although it is a resource everybody has, no one knows how much time you actually get.

In business, to achieve corporate goals you need four key components: people, materials, money and time. All require careful budgeting in order to be profitable. Organisations spend an enormous amount of their time monitoring the costs associated with staff and the materials required to function properly. Every penny is accounted for by the finance department to ensure maximum profitability. Audits are carried out on a regular basis so any misuse of funds is identified without delay and remedial action taken as quickly as possible.

However, one of the ingredients is unique and that is time. The other three – people, materials and money – can be replenished; if you need more you can always get them through various different outlets, such as borrowing or increasing sales. You can also, if required, hire additional staff or buy more materials, but with time, once it is gone you can't get it back.

Despite the fact that you cannot save up, borrow or buy additional time, people still misuse this priceless gift. People waste so much time worrying about things they have no control over, things that very often don't bring them happiness or value. People are slaves to the clock because they don't know how they actually spend their time. They allow situations and people to steal time from them despite the consequences. They live in a state of denial because they have bought into the myth, 'I know how I spend my time.' They are convinced they spend all of their working day being productive and that they are too busy to waste any time. However, just like John, they can see how others are continually wasting it.

Your memory is selective

How many times have you said at the end of a busy day, 'Where did that day go?' You spend much of the day on auto-pilot reacting to various demands and requests.

You know you're extremely busy but you are never quite sure how you actually spend your time. Your memory is selective and you only remember the productive or demanding tasks. Admitting to time-wasting is not a good career move so a working day is viewed in its best light. Long hours are confused with a good work ethic, which in turn is confused with being productive and profitable.

Staying late has become a habit and, instead of clearing your desk, it seems that you are as busy as ever. This can be explained by Parkinson's Law, which states, 'Work expands so as to fill the time available for its completion.' This saying was first attributed to Cyril Northcote Parkinson in the 1950s. Therefore it doesn't matter how long you stay in the office, as you will always find something to do.

However, to be a true master of your time, it is vital to understand how you really spend your time verses how you think you spend your time. This chapter is about establishing where your time is spent, where it is wasted, who steals most of your time (it could be you!) and what you can do about it.

The time you will spend analysing how you currently use your time is an investment in your future. You can't change anything about how you previously used your time, but you can use the information to strategically plan how you will use it in the future.

BUSINESS MANAGEMENT SKILLS – CONTROL

Time audit log

Henri Fayol believed that one of the key functions of management was control. In organisations around the world, it is the function of the finance department to monitor the way money is spent and collected. It ensures the financial resources are available so the organisation's goals can be achieved. It pulls together and analyses key information, which is then used to help management make day-to-day and strategic decisions. The same principles apply to managing yourself and how you use your time.

There are two important questions you must consider if you are serious about becoming a true master of your time:

- What would happen if you spent your money with as few safeguards as you spend your time?
- When was the last time you carried out a full and comprehensive review of how you really spend your time on a daily basis?

Keeping a time audit log, similar to a financial audit, will show you how you spend your time. It will identify the actual length of time it takes to complete important tasks instead of estimated times. It will also highlight key interruptions, whether they were value-added or not, and who interrupted you. It may even throw up some surprising facts for you to consider. But most of all it will bring you the key information you need in order to control how you use your time.

Why do you need safeguards with your time?

Time moves on whether you spend it foolishly or wisely. You can't control it but you can control how you use it. You must safeguard its use if you want to achieve what you really want from life. Money may be the lifeblood of an organisation but time is the air it breathes. The more you pollute and waste it, the more inefficient it becomes. Likewise, the more you pollute your time with toxic time-wasters, the less time you have available to do the things you should be doing.

Introducing safeguards to how you use your time will force you to think about each task in its entirety before you undertake it. It also ensures that you determine who and what is involved in its delivery. You need to have a clear understanding of what is involved before you start. This will help to eliminate potential non-value interruptions.

How to structure your time audit log

Conducting a thorough time audit requires discipline, honesty and persistence. The key point to remember is that this is your personal time audit and not a time sheet for management. There is no need to justify any activity you include in your audit. The aim is to quantify how you spend your time and not why you spend it in that particular fashion. You need to design your time audit log so that it captures all the relevant information about your day:

- Be clear
- Be honest
- Be concise
- Be complete

The idea of completing a time audit can be daunting. It is probably your first time to undertake such an activity, so it will naturally raise some questions. Where to start, the fear that it will take up too much time or reveal nothing are some of the reasons why very few people actually carry out time audits. However, a time audit is easy to complete and the benefits far outweigh any potential negatives. Keep your audit simple and build it up over time. As Lao-Tzu said, 'A journey of a thousand miles begins with a single step.' Try these suggested steps to start your time audit.

Step 1

Divide your day into representative blocks of time, for example, 15-minute or half-hour divisions. Then create seven columns as follows:

Hours	Planned activity	Actual activity	P	Interruption	C	Person
8:30						

The planned activity column is taken from your adding-value list. You simply transfer your daily plan to your audit log at the start of your audit period.

Step 2
Complete the log in real time, as remembering what you did several hours earlier can be very difficult. Be ruthless and record every activity change and any interruptions, no matter how small. The changes to your planned activities are recorded in the actual activity column and their priority level is highlighted in the column marked P. This will quickly establish if the changes are high priority or not. All interruptions are recorded (including any caused by yourself) with a brief note outlining what occurred. Keep this concise and meaningful. Classify the interruption into value added (V) or non-value added (NV). Finally, identify the source of the interruption and write the person's name and position in the person column.

Step 3
Ensure your log is with you at all times during the audit period to minimise the disruption of completing your log. It is a good idea to explain to your colleagues what you are doing and the reason why you are undertaking such a task. Some might surprise you and be very curious about your findings. If you gain buy-in from your colleagues it may help you to manage the source of your biggest disruptions.

Step 4
Review your log throughout the day to ensure there are no gaps in the timeline. It is important the information collected is complete and without bias. Remain focused and disciplined so that you will achieve the purpose of the time audit, which is to establish factually how you spend your time.

What should you put in a time audit?
The simple answer is to put absolutely everything you do in your time audit log. It is for your eyes only and not an instrument for management to use as a performance measure or a 'stick to beat you with' if you are under-performing. As mentioned earlier, this is not an exercise in justifying how you spend your time, it is about discovering how you truly do spend it.

Include routine tasks, hobby jobs, major projects, lunch breaks, meetings and even toilet breaks, as they all use time. Record how long every telephone conversation takes, all face-to-face conversations and even every time you daydream. The wider the scope of the data collected, the better your analysis will be. Be truthful with yourself as the only person you cannot fool is yourself. It is a personal voyage of discovery and self-awareness.

Being aware of how you actually spend your time opens the pathway to taking full responsibility for improving your use of time. You can only improve your performance in any business discipline if you are aware of both your strengths and weaknesses. Great business coaches talk about how unlocking your true potential requires an ability to be aware of the blocks that stand in your way of achieving peak performance.

'The essence of coaching is developing awareness and self-responsibility.'

Sir John Whitmore

Your personal time audit is your first opportunity to be totally frank and honest in assessing your work patterns, interruptions and blocks to peak performance. Time isn't a renewable resource so every misuse is a permanent debit. These debits or time losses will eventually bankrupt your performance levels if left unchecked.

What does your time log tell you?

Paul McGrath describes in his book *Back from the Brink* how alcohol affected his life and in particular his football career. He writes about how much time he lost through drink. He is not alone when it comes to people losing track of time due to alcohol and other vices. However, he says that a key question that must be asked is, 'How much time do you lose when sober?' A quick look at your time audit log will answer this question very quickly for you. Your log is an overview of how you have chosen to spend your time daily. It highlights the good and the wasteful activities.

The data collected in your time audit should be analysed at the end of each day – the longer you wait to review your findings, the less you will remember about it. Initially, conduct a simple analysis of the activities you have performed under these two headings:

- Achieved
- Time-wasters

Achieved. These are all the activities you've completed on time. Review the circumstances that ensured your success so this can be repeated again. Remember, you learn as much from your successes as your

Common time-wasters

- Telephone calls from non-customers
- Personal visitors
- Poor delegation skills, tasks you should have delegated
- Indecision – think about it, worry about it, and put it off
- IT problems
- Unclear objectives and priorities
- No plan for your day
- Doing urgent rather than important tasks
- Disorganised boss and colleagues
- Inadequate work supervision
- Being distracted by a messy desk
- Personal disorganisation, looking for things
- Unrealistic time estimates, managing people's expectations
- Miscommunication or poor communication methods
- Inefficiency
- Inadequate technical knowledge
- Procrastination
- Unnecessary errors
- Ineffective meetings
- Avoiding unpleasant tasks
- Lack of self-discipline
- Acting with incomplete information
- Dealing with team members
- Crisis management (firefighting)
- Unclear communication
- Stress and fatigue
- Inability to say no
- Travelling
- Revised deadlines

failures, and this is often overlooked in your quest for improvement. Identify key data that will help you in the future, such as:

- What part of the day were these successful activities completed?
- Did you have to manage any interruptions and, if so, what did you do?
- Was anyone else involved in the activity?
- Was it routine?
- What was its priority level?
- Who requested the activity?
- Can the positive working conditions be repeated?

Time-wasters. Most people like to claim they are too busy to waste any time and that time-wasters are no longer tolerated by organisations. However, the reality, whether you work in an office, a factory or in the home, is that you are consistently interrupted by phones, e-mails, colleagues and customers. Some of these interruptions are of high value (for example, customers buying more products or services), while others are of low or little value.

Research carried out by Gloria Mark of the University of California found that 'interruptions account for about 2.1 hours in an average worker's day' and that 'once interrupted, it can take up to 25 minutes to get back to your original task'. As you can see, it is not just the time wasted by the interruption itself that is a concern, but the length of time it can take to refocus on the original activity. It is this piece of information that puts the need to reduce interruptions into perspective.

Some of the most common reasons for reduced productivity and effectiveness in the workplace are listed in the margin. Review your audit log and draw up your own personal list of time-wasting activities. Compare your list to the one here and you might see that you have similar problems to most people.

The list, similar to your personal audit report, does not solve your problems; it merely reveals them. These are the practices that are getting in the way of your value-adding activities. Now the question is, can you eliminate them or at least rethink their usefulness and why you partake in them? You now need to focus on managing yourself and dealing with your biggest time-wasting activities.

Start by focusing your attention on the real issues, and the activities and practices you need to manage. You also have to accept that some interruptions are imposed on you and therefore you cannot influence or eliminate them. For example, your boss may call you into his office and urgently require an important report. Unfortunately, some people will waste even further time trying to manage these types of interruptions. The key is to accept them and try to reduce the impact they have on your working day.

A good practice is to initially manage the interruptions you can influence and, as you can see from the common list, there are in fact a number of areas you can manage easily and successfully. Always keep in mind your overall desire in wanting to be a master of your time.

Value or non-value?

Once you have highlighted all of the interruptions on your time audit report you should then classify them into adding value or adding no value. It is a simple but important process as it will give you a clearer picture of the non-value interruptions that need to go or be moved to a more convenient time. This list will become the focus of your managing yourself strategy.

Your list of non-value interruptions will include such things as smoking breaks, looking for missing files, colleagues dropping by unannounced for quick chats, and attending ineffective meetings. For the first time you will see very clearly how many interruptions you have each day, how much time is wasted on the non-value interruptions and who your biggest challenge is. Armed with this vital information, you can formulate some ideas on how you will start to eliminate or reduce your biggest problem areas.

Your audit records will also outline any patterns in your daily interruptions. This will help you with your scheduling of tasks when drawing up your adding-value lists. Remember to schedule non-urgent and important tasks when you are likely to have fewer interruptions, as these tasks will give you the greatest return on your time investment.

What to do with the information gathered in your time audit

After conducting your time audit and gathering key factual information, you need to prioritise your findings in order to make an impact on how you use your time. There is nothing more frustrating than spending time compiling a report for it to just sit on a shelf gathering dust and rapidly becoming out of date. Bill Gates writes in the opening paragraph of his book *Business @ the Speed of Thought* that 'how you gather, manage, and use information will determine whether you win or lose'.

'Many people think they want things, but they don't really have the strength, the discipline. They are weak. I believe that you get what you want if you want it badly enough.'

Sophia Loren

Time Audit Log

Day:

Hours	Planned activity	Actual activity	P	Interruption	C	Person
8:30						
9:00						
9:30						
10:00						
10:30						
11:00						
11:30						
12:00						
12:30						
1:00						
1:30						
2:00						
2:30						
3:00						
3:30						
4:00						
4:30						
5:00						
5:30						

Information is power, but how you use that information is even more powerful. Your report highlights the key time-wasting areas that need to be addressed. You must use this information to formulate a plan for showcasing your results to all the stakeholders within your organisation. Your stakeholders will play a role in your plan to improve how you use your time as some of them may be the biggest drain on your resources. You will have to manage both yourself and your stakeholders in order for your strategy to be successfully implemented. This next part will determine whether you remain a slave to the clock or become a master of your time.

Prioritising your report

How you deal with non-value interruptions can be captured on a simple-to-use prioritising grid as shown on the following page. The grid outlines the four options that determine your strategy for successful reduction of time-wasting activities. There are two key criteria to take into account when prioritising these activities – impact and influence.

Impact

The interruptions gathered on your time audit report have been divided into two categories: value adding and non-value adding. This is still a long list of interruptions, which could overwhelm you, leaving you with no idea of where to start. If this is the case, then it is a good idea to use Pareto's Principle again. Twenty per cent of your non-value interruptions will account for 80 per cent of your time-wasting activities. Prioritise your top time-wasting activities according to the amount of time wasted and not according to your personal preferences. These activities should be classed as high impact and the remaining activities classified as low impact.

Focus your attention on high-impact activities to start with as they have the biggest effect on the negative use of your time. For example, look for individuals who drop by for 'quick chats' and total the amount of time they steal from you. This could be a lot higher than you originally thought, particularly if they are someone who you interact with on a business level a lot or who you get on with well. Unless they are value-added, drop-bys should be managed ruthlessly.

Influence

Once you have listed the high-impact activities, the next step is to read your report again carefully and highlight the activities you have a lot of influence over. For example, identify the non-value interruptions caused by your own actions, such as phoning your friends or engaging in office gossip. These activities may be a welcome break from your daily tasks; however, they could be a major contributing factor to why you are missing deadlines or need to stay late to finish a report. In this example, your influence rating is high. Conversely, classify any activity you appear to have no control over as low.

Impact/influence grid

A Action now	B Be ruthless
C Can you influence?	D Don't waste any more time

Once you have labelled all of your non-adding-value interruptions as either high or low in relation to impact and influence, you can map them out on a grid like the one above. This is a snapshot of your time-wasting activities and it allows you to see very quickly where your focus should be in order to improve your productivity.

According to the Global Productivity Study carried out by Proudfoot Consulting, the majority of businesses across the world currently operate at productivity levels of between 50 and 60 per cent. This means that employees are also working at reduced capacity. The study found that poor management in terms of planning and control and day-to-day supervision was the biggest factor in lost time. By establishing the root cause of your time-wasting activities you can start the process of improving your performance by being proactive in managing problem areas rather than reacting to them. Your time-wasting activities require close supervision or else they can get out of control rapidly.

Using the impact/influence grid will help to establish which quadrant your time-wasting activities belong in and therefore where your priority management should focus. It clearly outlines the activities you have control over and those you have limited control over.

Time-wasting activities that have both a high impact and high influence rating should be in **Quadrant A**. These are the high-priority tasks that require immediate managing and the introduction of processes to eliminate them. Every activity that is eliminated from Quadrant A greatly increases your productivity level.

Quadrant A deals with the activities you can influence the most and that steal the most time from you. These are the high-impact and high-influence activities that make you less productive, such as surfing websites, poor delegation and completing non-value hobby jobs. A simple analysis of these activities will show you how much time you are spending in this quadrant. If these activities are minimised, the effect on your performance will be dramatic. They are also the easiest tasks to eliminate completely as they only require self-management. Set a clear target to reduce the number of activities in this quadrant and analyse the impact it has on your time.

Masters of time replace Quadrant A activities with Green Priority C time activities from their adding-value lists. This is a key strategic move as it maximises the use of lost time by replacing the time-wasting activities with important but not urgent activities. This simple management principle will greatly improve your results as you spend more time working on important tasks before they become fire-fighting tasks.

As you discovered in the last chapter, the more time you allocate to Green Priority C tasks, the less tasks fall into the Red Zone and will develop into crises. Stephen Covey, in his book *The Seven Habits of Highly Effective People*, puts it,

> Your effectiveness would increase dramatically. Your crises and problems would shrink to manageable proportions because you would be thinking ahead, working on the roots, doing the preventive things that keep situations from developing into crises in the first place. In time management jargon, this is called the Pareto Principle – 80 percent of the results flow out of 20 percent of activities.

Quadrant B deals with activities you also have a great deal of influence over but the impact on the amount of time these activities waste is not as big as those in Quadrant A. They are low-impact and high-influence activities. Unfortunately, if they are left unchecked for any length of time then they too can become a major problem area. Some of the Quadrant B activities include indecision, disorganised work stations, and doing urgent rather than important tasks.

Although the impact on your time is small, Quadrant B activities shouldn't be overlooked because if you add them all up you might find that they are wasting a significant amount of time. These time-wasting activities can also surface repeatedly during the day, such as phone calls from friends. Each call may only last five minutes, but there could be six or seven of them a day, which means you could be wasting up to three hours per week. The key here is to be ruthless before they become a problem.

In **Quadrant C** you will list the activities that are high on impact but low on influence. These are the activities that can frustrate you greatly and they are usually the things you complain about the loudest. The fact that they are outside your control means that you highlight them the most. They are chiefly the excuses you use when deadlines are missed, long hours are clocked up and productivity is down. Time-wasting activities in Quadrant C include a disorganised boss, non-sales phone calls from customers and going to ineffective meetings.

On the surface these activities appear to be outside your control. However, like all activities, they need to be managed. Instead of locking them into the 'can't influence' quadrant, the key is to keep asking the question, 'How can I influence these activities?' After all, they have a high-impact rating, so they greatly reduce your productivity. Some of the solutions may lie in the fact that many of these activities involve other people, such as customers and managers.

Finally, in **Quadrant D** you will find the tasks that are low on impact and low on influence. The key here is not to waste any further time on them. Deal with them as they arise and then move on quickly to other activities. Sometimes finding the solution to eliminate an activity will take up more time than the original activity wasted in the first place.

In reality, prioritising an audit report will vary from person to person as some people will rate certain time-wasting activities higher than others. The exercise can suffer from being too subjective as there can be more grey areas than simple black-and-white decisions. However, it is important you rate your time-wasting activities so that key areas are not overlooked. Use the various combinations of impact and influence to decide whether an enslaving activity is rated as high or low.

In the next chapter you will use the impact/influence grid to manage non-value interruptions effectively by placing each interruption into one of the four quadrants. Take your time when creating this grid as it will form the basis of your plan of attack to deal with time-wasting activities.

Cost your time

Once you have completed the impact/influence grid, you need to cost out each of the interruptions you have listed. Beside each activity you have already recorded the amount of time used. Now simply calculate the cost of these interruptions by using your hourly rate. This will reveal the true cost of each interruption to your organisation.

For instance, if you earn €20 per hour and you are wasting two hours per day, then on average you could be costing your organisation up to €10,000 per annum due to non-value activities. If there are eight people in your team with the same time-wasting habits, then your organisation could be losing €80,000 per annum.

Showcasing your results

Promote your results and overcome any resistance to change, whether it is internally (yourself) or externally (other people). After all it is your time that is being wasted. Set yourself a target of how many time-wasting activities you are going to eliminate from your working environment and thereby increase your productivity levels. The key is planning (adding-value list) and control (time audit).

Identify the important stakeholders who are connected to you as they will influence the implementation of your action plan. Involve them early in the process so they feel part of your development. Give some small incentives to your stakeholders to encourage their positive participation.

What does your time audit achieve?

A time audit enables you to adjust a key resource to accommodate your changing and demanding business environment. It is a health check, which ensures you are in good shape and that you have the factual data required to be a master of your time. It enhances your ability to manage yourself and how you use your time by setting realistic expectations of what can be achieved in your working day. It also helps you to make decisions about how to approach your strategy for reducing non-value interruptions.

The Global Productivity Study carried out by Proudfoot Consulting found 'that poor management in terms of planning and control and day-to-day supervision was the biggest factor in lost time'. A time audit gives you the raw data that underpins good planning and control as it provides essential information to help you schedule your adding-value lists so that you can maximise the time available to you. It reveals the threats and opportunities you face on a daily basis.

It also highlights issues that may be outside your circle of influence – organisational issues, such as badly designed work flows, or some basic management skills your boss is missing.

A time audit is the bedrock on which you can build your future working environment. It provides you with an accurate assessment of your present use of time. Without this clear understanding it would be very difficult to introduce your vision for the future. Ken Blanchard and Jesse Stoner illustrate this point perfectly when they state, 'Vision without being present is like having your head in the clouds. Holding the present without vision is like being stuck in the mud.' They go on to say in their book *Full Steam Ahead* that 'Doing both – focusing on your vision and being honest about the truth of your present situation – is what allows you to move full steam ahead.' A time audit concentrates your mind on achieving tangible results in your quest to be a master of time.

Regular reviews

Personal time audits are extremely beneficial to a master of time. They provide invaluable data, which is used to formulate your strategy for managing yourself and your stakeholders. Write a mission statement for your time audit to define its overall purpose. Keep it simple and concise, no more than two or three sentences. The mission statement will create the desired results for your time audit. Print it out and hang it in a prominent place. This will inform your stakeholders that you are serious about getting rid of time-wasters.

Your time audit is not a one-off event. Good management practice dictates you carry out a time audit every quarter. This will help you to discover if there are any changes to your working habits, whether they are good or bad. It is important to see if you are replacing old time-wasting activities with other non-value tasks instead of value-adding tasks. Also, complacency can set in after your initial enthusiasm for change.

Spot a slave

Slaves to the clock love playing the victim. It is the easy route where they don't take responsibility for their inaction. Why should they, as they can blame someone else for all of their misfortune? It is always someone else who does the time-wasting. They didn't make the decision to carry out a time audit in the first place so therefore they weren't responsible for its outcome. If they were coerced into doing this futile exercise (after all, they never waste time as they are too busy), they produced time sheets and not a time audit report.

They adopt a cynical view of time audits. According to slaves to the clock, time audits are a way in which management will look to get even more work out of them. They believe that management will use the data to benchmark all of the staff and thereby to make them work longer and harder.

Slaves to the clock like to keep the status quo and work within their comfort zone. They have never completed a time audit in the past, so why start now? Fear of the results, perhaps!

Playing the victim card is not a healthy option if you really want to change how you use your time. In *Flight of the Buffalo*, James A. Belasco and Ralph C. Stayer tell people that 'Being a victim is a danger to our success, and there's always something we can do to get better control over virtually any situation.'

Spot the master

A master of time takes the necessary actions to achieve great performance and, in doing so, they remove the barriers that stand in their path. They use the data gathered in time audits to remove their time-wasting activities. They make things happen as they focus on the doing rather than the talking. They understand the true value of their time. They are not cynics, as Oscar Wilde so eloquently portrayed in *Lady Windermere's Fan*: 'What is a cynic? A man who knows the price of everything and the value of nothing.'

Dos and don'ts of time audits

Do: Be a master
- Keep accurate notes on key interruptions
- Be honest and record every time-wasting activity
- Ruthlessly weed out tasks that are non-value
- Take responsibility for your actions
- Conduct regular audits

Don't: Be a slave
- Be selective with your entries into your log
- Jump to quick conclusions about how your time is wasted
- Blame others
- Agree with the findings but then fail to change your habits

INTRODUCING MASTER OF TIME TO THE HOME

There never seems to be enough time to do all the things you need to do. After spending a hectic week at work, the weekend becomes a battle zone as conflicting activities fight for your time. Should you catch up with the cleaning or spend time with the children? Should you organise your clothes for next week or indulge in your hobby? Should you visit family and friends or finish the DIY project? Now more than ever time has become a real issue for people.

'Our ambition should be to rule ourselves, the true kingdom for each one of us; and true progress is to know more, and be more, and to do more.'

Oscar Wilde

Effective time management skills develop over time with practise and monitoring. To improve the quality use of your time at home you must complete a time audit. You need to weed out your time-wasting activities and the best way to start this process is to establish how you really spend your time. Record the everyday jobs you are doing and the length of time you spend on each one. Also include your energy levels, whether they are high or low. Continue this audit for at least two weeks. This should give you a clearer picture of how you spend your time. Rate each task as follows:

- Must be done, otherwise disaster
- Should be done to keep everything running smoothly
- Would be nice if it was done but fine anyway
- Someone else could do this for me

Once you have completed this audit you can see if you are spending your time wisely. Your report should answer some basic questions:

- Who and what are my main time-wasters?
- What everyday jobs take the longest time to finish?
- Are there quicker ways of completing these tasks?
- What are my hobby jobs?
- When are my energy levels at their optimum?
- What tasks should I be concentrating on during my peak levels?

The purpose of the audit is not to ensure that you account for every minute of your day. It is to establish you are spending it the way you would like to spend it. Are you doing the activities that bring you joy, happiness and excitement? What activities are causing you stress? Is there enough time for relaxation in your life?

Your personal time audit will highlight the time-wasting activities you succumb to. Once they have been established, you can eliminate them by using the same techniques you apply to your work schedule. You can also replace these activities with exciting new hobbies and fun experiences with your family and friends. There will be no more 'I haven't got the time' excuses for not doing the things that bring you happiness and joy.

Before you read any further, take a break and write down the next part of your plan.

'Rest is not idleness, and to lie sometimes on the grass under trees on a summer's day, listening to the murmur of the water, or watching the clouds float across the sky, is by no means a waste of time.'

J. Lubbock

PERSONAL THOUGHTS

What will I do differently tomorrow?

MYTH NO. 4
I CAN'T CONTROL INTERRUPTIONS

YOU ARE HAEMORRHAGING TIME

The theory behind moving to an open-plan office environment is simple; it improves communication channels between co-workers and between workers and management. People are free to talk easily without having to move too far from their desk. This informality allows fast communication in all directions and speeds up the decision-making process. Its openness also invites people to drop by and ask for help on work-related issues without making appointments and to seek opinions on the best course of action with a difficult task. The concept of open-plan working is to improve the interaction between colleagues and thereby to improve productivity within the organisation.

For John, the improvement in his communication with his colleagues has been evidenced since he moved into his plush new open-plan surroundings. His desk is conveniently positioned beside the coffee machine, which means there is a constant stream of people passing him to get their hourly caffeine fix. Most of his co-workers assume John is in charge of the coffee machine and turn to him if it is out of cups or coffee. They also seem to think that he is there to provide them with interesting conversation as they wait for their coffee. Affable John, keen to be the team-player, is now suffering the side effects of an open-plan working area. Saying no to these unscheduled interruptions and time-wasting activities is not strong point and as a result he is very likely to be heard engaged in office banter, gossip and wasteful activities. He has also taken on the unofficial title of 'coffee supplies co-ordinator'.

'It has been my observation that most people get ahead during the time that others waste.'

Henry Ford

61

A typical scene from his daily routine unfolds as follows:

'Hi John, did you see the match last night – great result, wasn't it?' enquired Barry, as he made his customary latte. 'Oh, do you know where the sugar is?'

'Yeah, it was a terrific game, the better team definitely won,' replied John as he stopped inputting the sales figures, leaned back into his chair and pointed to the sugar on the top shelf.

'Oh yeah, I see it now. We were class alright, what do you think of our chances of going all the way this season?'

'I suppose if we don't do it this year we'll never do it. We have the best team we've had in years. Listen, I'm up to my eyes at the moment with this report. I'll…'

'I know the feeling John, I'm swamped myself. Tell me something – you're a bit of an expert on team selection, who would you play up front when we have all our guys back from injury?'

'Tough one that, I know we're really spoilt for choice up front. It's the defence I'm worried about. I think we have…'

This conversation went on for another 15 minutes as the two lads argued over the merits of each front player and who they would buy as a defender if they were in charge of the team. During this time no work was discussed, completed or thought about, although both had claimed to be extremely busy. As the discussions intensified, Rory, a big sport fan, peered over his partition and joined in the debate.

Now there was a three-way conversation taking place until the phone interrupted them. Rachel, the sales manager, was checking to see if John had put through this month's expense forms for the sales reps.

John, frustrated that he had to stop a passionate debate with his colleagues, curtly replied, 'Look, Rachel, I'm in the middle of inputting them at the moment so if you stop checking up on me I'll have them through.'

These wasteful interruptions are a common occurrence in most working and social environments. The subject matter may differ, but these sorts of conversations happen frequently. The average amount of your time that haemorrhages each day with similar interruptions can be calculated from your analysis of your time audit. It should make interesting reading. Now that you know the root source of your time draining away, you need to begin operating on these causes.

BUSINESS MANAGEMENT SKILLS – COMMANDING

Another key managerial function, according to Henri Fayol, is commanding. It involves giving instructions to get the job done. When instructions are given and timeframes agreed, it is expected that the tasks are completed on time. This is the principle by which organisations are run. However, management often fail to take into consideration a key fact that will affect the timeframes agreed upon – interruptions.

Interruptions are a fact of life in all organisations. Non-value interruptions are a source of much time-wasting. Some people are good at dealing with these interruptions, while others allow interruptions to dictate their workflow and suffer missed deadlines as a consequence. Top performers avoid time-killer activities by taking control of the situation. One of the methods they use, according to Robert E. Kelly, is to

> adopt behaviours that allow them to minimise interruptions in their workday without separating them from the group. For example, they will often take a 'working vacation' – escaping to another part of the office to complete work.

Focus on what you can influence

Shift the blame for missing deadlines due to overwork to the correct culprit, which is non-value interruptions and the length of time it takes to refocus onto the task at hand after them. Every time you are interrupted, it is adding to the time it takes to complete the task you were working on. Controlling non-value interruptions requires an unemotional approach similar to that of a surgeon. Swiftly and clinically, you remove any cancerous time-wasting activities before it is too late and you have lost the ability to function productively.

> 'It's not the time it takes to take the takes that takes the time; it's the time it takes between the takes that takes the time.'
>
> Steven Spielberg

The 'I can't control interruptions' slaves are everywhere. They allow the non-value interruptions to control their lives. They feel helpless and overwhelmed. They do not believe that they can control the volume of interruptions that steal their time. As a result, they frequently miss deadlines and work under constant stress. They are nice people who have difficulty saying no. Colleagues drop by unannounced and have no problems stealing their time. They participate in endless non-value conversations, which ultimately mean they end up staying late in order to complete their tasks. They also have a habit of coming in early when it is quiet because 'there are no interruptions'.

> 'The person who says it cannot be done should not interrupt the person doing it.'
>
> Chinese proverb

If you can relate to the problems that 'I can't control interruptions'

When was the last time you did this?

Ask yourself two revealing questions that will help you deal with non-value interruptions:

- How many 'drop by' interruptions do you get each day?
- Do you know what time of day you get most of them?

slaves encounter, then you must take control of the situation now. You need to focus on what you can do, not on what you can't. Dealing with interruptions requires decisive action. In their book *Who are 'They' Anyway?*, B.J. Gallagher and Steve Ventura talk about focusing your energy and attention on the things you can influence and change, not on the things you have no control over. They say,

> The simplest way to do this is to frequently ask yourself: 'Is there something I can do about this problem? In what ways can I contribute to the solution?' Sometimes the answer will be a clear 'yes'- and sometimes it will be a clear 'no.' But be careful, for sometimes that 'no' is simply habit, a way of looking at the world that says: 'I have no power here – those things are out of my control.'

Maybe, as Gallagher and Ventura say, you have more control over reducing the non-value interruptions than you think. In the last chapter the impact/influence grid was introduced to give you a snapshot of your time-wasting activities and it allowed you see very quickly where your focus should be in order to improve your productivity.

Impact/influence grid

A Action now	B Be ruthless
C Can you influence?	D Don't waste any more time

Quadrant A deals with the activities you can influence the most and that steal the most time from you. These are the non-value interruptions you must deal with immediately, such as 'drop bys' and non-value phone calls.

Quadrant B deals with activities you also have a great deal of influence over but the amount of time these activities waste is not as big as those in Quadrant A. They are low-impact and high-influence activities; however, they can mount up if they are not dealt with as they arise. Be ruthless with this type of interruption too.

In **Quadrant C** you find the activities that are high on impact but low on influence. These are the activities that can frustrate you greatly, and they are usually the things you complain about the loudest. The fact that they are outside your control means you highlight them the most.

In **Quadrant D** you find the tasks that are low on impact and low on influence. The key here is not to waste any further time on them. Deal with them as they arise and then move on quickly to other activities.

The impact/influence grid usually reveals that you have more control over your non-value interruptions than you would have acknowledged at first. A master of their time uses the grid to tackle the high-impact and high-influence interruptions first, before expending any energy on dealing with high-impact, low-influence activities. You will use the impact/influence grid later in this chapter to deal with non-value interruptions.

Take a risk

Maybe being a slave to interruptions is your comfort zone and breaking free carries too many risks. But taking risks is not necessarily a bad thing because great changes nearly always involve some element of risk. However, there is a world of difference between flying off to Las Vegas to bet your entire savings on a twist of a card and managing interruptions. There is a trade-off between risk and reward.

> 'A life spent making mistakes is not only more honourable but more useful than a life spent in doing nothing.'
>
> George Bernard Shaw

Dealing with the risks associated with managing interruptions is a straightforward process. A successful risk-management strategy is about assessing the probability that a loss or negative outcome will occur, and the potential cost of the loss if it was to occur. Sometimes it is even more straightforward to analyse the consequences of not taking action and the potential loss of adapting this strategy. Failure to manage interruptions will cost you time, and the time-stealers will continue to drain your limited resource.

Create new habits

Hyrum W. Smith explains:

> We are all creatures of habit, whether we like it or not. Even though the inertia of habits often keeps us in our comfort zone instead of reaching our goals, habits per se are not necessarily bad. In fact, life would be a nightmare without habits. We would have to make conscious decisions at every turn. Nothing would be automatic.

He goes on to pose a key question about the power of habits: 'Am I willing to develop good habits or am I content to develop bad ones?'

Allowing distractions to control your working day is a bad habit, which you have allowed to take root over a period of time. Every day you are bombarded with information and your natural curiosity and a desire to be available will ensure you are distracted. In her article entitled 'Getting Out from Under' for *Fortune Magazine*, Ellen McGirt wrote:

> The peoples of the earth sent and received 400,000 terabytes of information by e-mail in 2002, according to research by the University of California at Berkeley's School of Information Management and Systems. That's equivalent to the print collections of 40,000 Libraries of Congress. As for phone calls – which accounted for some 17 million terabytes of information in 2002 – now they can follow us everywhere.

How much of that information is value-adding and how much is non-value is impossible to know. However, what is known about slaves to the clock is that they allow themselves to be distracted by this information juggernaut and waste between two and three hours per day reacting to non-value interruptions. They allow bad habits to dictate how they use their time. Slaves feel the need to be responsive and believe that being available all the time is a positive trait. They see this as being an efficient worker and showing a willingness to be team player. Those may be correct beliefs for some professionals such as fire-fighters and the police force, but for most workers this habit of being available all the time could be counter-productive. The challenge in today's environment is balancing being available with doing what you should be doing, which is to add value to yourself and your organisation.

Excellent business practice is about achieving this balance and eliminating the many distractions that don't add value. Building the discipline to ignore non-value distractions requires strength and the conviction that you are doing the right thing. In *The Principles of Psychology*, American philosopher William James wrote, 'The art of being wise is the art of knowing what to overlook.' By ignoring the tasks that don't have a negative consequence if they are not completed, you will start to chip away at the 25 per cent of your day that is wasted. One of Socrates' often-quoted maxims is, 'We are what we repeatedly do. Excellence, then, is a habit.' Overlooking non-value tasks must become one of your daily habits. Excellence is achieved through a willingness to be ruthless with time-wasters.

Change to winning habits

In today's business environment people and organisations are experiencing change at an ever-increasing rate in order to stay competitive.

These changes take on many different guises, including procedural changes, mergers between organisations, restructuring within organisations or simply introducing new technology. Whatever the type of change taking place, it is important it is implemented successfully and with as little disruption to people and work production as possible. Although this is a major challenge for those entrusted with the task of implementing change, there are some simple principles that can reduce the stress and risk of failure associated with changes. The same rules and approaches apply when you undertake the challenge to change how you use your time and cope with non-value interruptions.

Changing the way you manage these interruptions requires you not only to survive one major change in your approach to mastering your time, but also to be able to deal with repeated changes because your list of interruptions is long and diverse. To be successful and to implement your strategy in a positive way, you must learn from the experience of each change.

'When the rate of change inside an organisation is slower than the rate of change outside the organisation, the end is in sight.'
John Welsh, former chairman, General Electric

'Excellent firms don't believe in excellence, only in constant improvement and constant change.'
Tom Peters, co-author of
In Search of Excellence

Structure your approach to change

Breaking old habits is hard but not impossible. As outlined in the first chapter, you must have a desire and commitment to change and develop a winning mindset. Your first critical step towards becoming a true master of your time was to set your 'best way to use my time' goal. This goal is now the driving force behind your quest for improving the way you use your time and turning your vision into the way you manage your life. When you set yourself this goal, there were two elements that determined whether you would be successful: a clear understanding of the goal, and the motivation to achieve it. The technique outlined to achieve this result was setting goals using the SMARTER Way Goal Setting System™.

This technique can be incorporated into your change strategy. You are responsible for the consequences of your actions (or inaction), which means you can implement immediately your desired changes to the way in which you deal with non-value interruptions. Developing a framework that outlines the various steps required to successfully implement your plans can help reduce the stress and frustration normally associated with such changes. Employing a systematic approach allows you to concentrate on building new habits. Use the CHANGE Model™ as follows:

'Winning is not a sometime thing; it's an all time thing. You don't win once in a while, you don't do things right once in a while, you do them right all the time. Winning is habit. Unfortunately, so is losing.'
Vince Lombardi

C	Choose
H	How
A	Align
N	No
G	Gain
E	Experience

Choose

The first step in the CHANGE Model™ is to choose the non-value interruption you want to manage. As discussed in the last chapter, it is beneficial to use the impact/influence grid to establish which interruption you should focus on initially. Achieving quick wins will encourage a culture of change and a winning mentality.

Spending time deciding on which interruptions to manage and in which order to do so can save you lots of time and wasted energy. Quadrant A activities are the interruptions you can influence the most and that steal the most time from you. These are the high-impact and high-influence activities that make you less productive. Quadrant A activities include non-value interruptions such as personal phone calls, unscheduled breaks, reading e-mails every time they pop up on your screen and unnecessary drop-bys. If you focus your energy on changing your habits in dealing with these interruptions, the effect on your overall performance will be dramatic. They are also the easiest tasks to eliminate completely as you can control them directly. Use the SMARTER Way Goal Setting System™ to drive your strategy forward and to maintain improvements achieved.

Set a clear target to reduce the number of activities in Quadrant A and analyse the impact it has on your time. Calculate how much time you now have available for other tasks. A good business practice is to replace the time wasted on Quadrant A activities with non-urgent and important tasks. This will allow you to spend more time adding real value to you, your career and your organisation. When you have completed Quadrant A activities, then move on to Quadrant B and repeat the process. For most people, if you can eliminate Quadrant A and Quadrant B activities from your daily schedule, then you will be in control of your work.

How

A clear vision of where the changes will take you and how you will get there is a critical step in the change process. Being visionary means you will sometimes need to step away from the crowd and do what is best for you and your organisation. A lot of wasteful interruptions are caused by you and your peers. This means you will have to make some tough decisions in order to achieve your goals. Therefore, always start with the end result clearly envisaged.

If you are travelling somewhere for the first time you will probably consult a roadmap before you leave to ensure that you reach the correct destination. The same principle applies to people undergoing change. Creating new habits means many difficult choices will have to be made on your journey. Outline the various options available and don't automatically choose the easiest path. You must pick your route carefully and you will then achieve great results. In the final verse of Robert Frost's poem 'The Road Not Taken' he reflects that the obvious choice is not always the best one:

> I shall be telling this with a sigh
> Somewhere ages and ages hence:
> Two roads diverged in a wood, and I –
> I took the one less traveled by,
> And that has made all the difference.

Write a clear roadmap for change that doesn't include any ambiguities. Leave out any sentences that contain the words 'should' or 'might' as they suggest that that idea is optional. For example, 'I should complete an impact/influence matrix,' or, 'I might eliminate one interruption this week,' show a lack of conviction in your roadmap. Maybe there is a better route. Do you really want to go there? Your roadmap should inspire confidence that these changes are necessary, well thought-out and will be successfully implemented. Your roadmap displays your strength of character and your commitment to being a master of time.

Your roadmap should be detailed, with clearly outlined milestones to check your progress. It is your blueprint for success.

Align

There can be lots of complexities when introducing any form of change. Dealing with interruptions may involve overcoming a range of challenges and several different people. As a result, there could be many

Your roadmap must contain the following information:

- Your desired destination – what non-value interruptions you are changing and how you will know if you are successful
- List the options available to you and then select which one you will take
- The length of time it will take to implement the change and get to your destination
- Your first move and your final move
- The people who will support you on your journey
- Any potential barriers you need to overcome
- Your contingency plan for dealing with those barriers

small changes taking place at once, which may be interdependent. You must introduce a system to track all of your changes to ensure there are no delays or duplication. Each change needs to be linked and monitored as your strategy develops.

It is useful to draw a map of the changes you are implementing and link changes that are dependent on each other. This will help you decide which sequence your journey should take, and also provide you with some road-marking to track your progress. Document all the changes you are undertaking so that none are forgotten.

No news is bad news

Whenever change is taking place, there is an element of fear attached. You are breaking out of your comfort zone and are unsure of what the future might bring. The risks associated with the changes are often overstated or exaggerated. A number of questions, which can't be answered, surface:

- Will the changes work?
- What do you do if they don't succeed?
- Will you end up in a worse position than the one you were in before you started the change process?

These are genuine concerns and must be addressed.

Therefore, communication, whether it is good news or bad, is better than no news at all when you are undergoing change. Even if the changes only involve you, it is a great idea to hold a quick debriefing session to assess your progress. If there are other stakeholders involved, keep them informed at all times. These regular and well-targeted communication briefing sessions are essential for the success of this change project.

Feedback from the stakeholders on how they are coping with your changes is also important, as it can often be the source of useful data and suggestions. The changes you have launched may be working very well for you personally but could be a disaster for your team. For example, you might have introduced a closed-door policy where you are not to be disturbed for two hours. This has proved to be extremely beneficial to you, but your team has found it to be unworkable because you are the only person who can authorise discounts to customers. As you work in a highly competitive market, your customers expect an answer immediately. Because of your closed-door policy these discount confirmations can be delayed by up to two hours, which has resulted in lost sales. Clearly this change is not feasible.

Gain

Gaining commitment from all stakeholders is an important stage in implementing your changes. It can speed up the process because some of the interruptions you are eliminating affect not only you, but also other stakeholders. Some are caused by them and they need to be part of the solution. Underestimating the power that stakeholders have in the success of your change strategy can be fatal.

The first step to take to gain buy-in is to identify all stakeholders directly involved in your strategy for change. Keep this list as broad as possible as they are all potential time-wasters. Then you need to establish their reaction to the changes you wish to implement. This is achieved by asking quality questions. It is best to use open questions as you want them to explain their position. When thinking about the type of questions you are going to ask, remember it is your stakeholder who has the answers. Therefore it is wise to avoid closed questions as they rarely give you the information you're looking for. They are also known as lazy questions as they do the thinking for the person who is answering them.

When you receive a positive reaction to your plans from a stakeholder, turn them into a champion. A champion is your friend who will support you through this change process. They can be very influential, particularly if your champion is in a senior or powerful position. Enlist your champions to persuade other stakeholders that your changes will benefit them.

However, if you start to get any negative reactions you must deal with them as early as possible as others could be poisoned by their viewpoint. Meet with them on a one-to-one basis and revisit the benefits of your plan from their point of view only. It is their benefits you need to articulate, not yours. Ask good, open questions to establish their reasons for rejecting your strategy. The more information you gather, the easier it will be to convince them your plan will be beneficial to both parties.

At first they maybe sceptical so you need to focus on the end result. Paint the full picture as seen through their eyes. Outline how they will profit from the improvement in the way you use your time. You need to clearly outline what is in it for them if they reduce the number of times they interrupt you. Show them how much of your time is lost daily through non-value interruptions and that if you can reduce this wastage then they will also improve their productivity. Deal with their concerns one at a time. Ensure that each concern is overcome before moving on to the next issue.

Experience

As outlined earlier, when you are changing the way in which you deal with non-value interruptions, you are in fact undergoing repeated changes.

There is more than one interruption to remove. It is good management practice to undertake a thorough debriefing session during the change process as it will provide you with vital information on how successful you are at implementing the changes.

Be sure you don't end up trying to re-invent the wheel; if someone else has successfully reduced or eliminated similar interruptions to yours, see if their strategy would work for you. You don't have to go through the hard work of trying to figure out the best way to deal with interruptions on your own. The great thing about your journey to being a master of time is that you are not alone. Others have walked the well-worn path to discovery; some successfully, while others gave up when they neared the finish line.

Experience is about learning from your and other people's past to influence your future. It is about assessing what went wrong and changing your strategy accordingly. Experience is also about learning from your successes. This is often overlooked, but it can be the source of great knowledge. Continually do the things that you are good at and build on your successes.

Influencing those who steal your time

It is one thing to know what to do but another to go ahead and do it. Developing your strategy for creating new habits is your plan; implementing it determines your success. Dealing with interruptions depends on your ability to influence both yourself and those who steal your time.

Influencing is a key leadership skill. Great world figures like Nelson Mandela, Bill Clinton, Bill Gates, Gandhi, Mother Teresa, JFK, Martin Luther King, Jr, and many others used the power of influence to take their vision and change the world. You can take your power to influence and change your world and become a master of your time. You can change the way you work so that you can reduce the time stolen from you through endless interruptions. You can influence your time bandits.

The power of influence is your ability to gain commitment from other people to a particular point of view, to persuade people that a specific course of action is right. It allows you to achieve more control over how you use your time during the day. Your ability to influence will help you to state your case in a convincing manner when you start to deal with wasteful interruptions. It will help you to convince your colleagues that your vision for the future will benefit them as well as you, that dealing with non-value interruptions is the way forward. You can influence other people's behaviour and actions in a positive way that will reduce non-value interruptions for them also.

An important ingredient in persuading people to do what you what them to do is to give a reason why you want something done. Robert B. Cialdini, in his book *Influence: The Psychology of Persuasion*, talks about an experiment carried out by a Harvard social psychologist, Ellen Langer, to explain how people are conditioned to act in certain ways. He says:

> A well known principle of human behaviour says that when we ask someone to do us a favor we will be more successful if we provide a reason. People simply like to have reasons for what they do. Langer demonstrated this unsurprising fact by asking a small favor of people waiting in a line to use a library copying machine: 'Excuse me, I have five pages. May I use the Xerox machine because I'm in a rush?' The effectiveness of this request-plus-reason was nearly total: Ninety-four per cent of those asked let her skip ahead of them in line.

Another factor to consider before you implement your strategy for change is to realise that not everyone will be influenced simply because you gave them an explanation. You need to tailor the reason why they should do something to suit the needs of each individual. How people are influenced is shaped by their personality, motivation and perception. As a result, most people will think differently to you, make decisions differently to you, use their time differently to you, have different work patterns and be motivated differently to you.

There are different types of slaves to the clock – seven in total – who steal time from you through their non-value interruptions. Each can be influenced by tailoring your approach to meet their needs. If you can identify the type of slave you need to deal with, then it will increase your success rate. The seven slaves are Talkative Slaves, Indecisive Slaves, I Want it Now Slaves, Haphazard Slaves, Let's Have Harmony Slaves, Leave it 'Til Tomorrow Slaves and No Plan Slaves. Each slave displays behaviour you need to manage carefully. Some of the stakeholders who steal your time may engage in behaviours displayed by more than one slave.

'If there is any one secret of success, it lies in the ability to get the other person's point of view and see things from that person's angle as well as from your own.'
Henry Ford

Talkative Slaves

Some people are high on talkative energy. They like to talk to people and are energised by the interaction between people. Talkative Slaves have a habit of using the opening tag line of 'Have you got a minute?' and proceeding to launch into a conversation before you have had time to answer their initial question. Have you ever experienced anyone leaving your office after a minute when they open with that dreaded phrase? It is perhaps one of the greatest and most widely used lies of all time. It is even more problematic if the person is extremely outgoing and sociable. Their minute often becomes 15 or 20, all of which are stealing time from you.

Talkative Slaves can be hard to ignore as they are high on enthusiasm, like having fun while working, and are eager to talk to their colleagues at every opportunity. Time-keeping isn't one of their strengths, particularly when it comes to meetings. However, they do embrace change and are willing to express their opinions. They don't particularly like a lot of paperwork or filling out forms, and tend to be challenged by new tasks rather than repetitive activities. They seek out feedback from their colleagues and like to work with other people.

Talkative Slaves are prone to think out loud. They say the first thing that comes into their head without thinking about the consequences. Debating issues is their preferred mechanism for decision-making as they like to include everyone in the process.

How to influence a Talkative Slave

- Always allow some time for social interaction before coming to the real purpose of the conversation – you may disengage the Talkative Slave if you cut to the chase too quickly
- Describe your vision to them using positive language; get them to picture the outcome
- Use paraphrasing and clarifying questions to control the length and direction of the conversation
- Encourage the completion of a written action plan in order to monitor progress, as Talkative Slaves often over-promise what they can deliver
- If possible, schedule the meeting in their office or at their desk so you can have an exit plan
- Ensure there is a sense of enjoyment in the interaction to maintain the interest of a Talkative Slave; don't be too formal
- Diplomacy is often required when you haven't time to interact

with a Talkative Slave. Set them a timeframe at the start of the conversation, which will help to manage their expectations. Use excuses like, 'I have a meeting with the finance director in ten minutes so we can either talk now quickly or reschedule for 5:15.'

• Use inspirational quotes to galvanise their commitment

Indecisive Slaves

According to John Adair, there are two definitions of decision.

> By one extreme definition almost everything we do involves making decisions; by another, at the other end of the scale, we make only a few real decisions in our lives. The first school of opinion would hold that a manager spends almost all his time decision making; the second school declares that he makes few real decisions, but that they are highly significant events.

Whether it is the sheer volume of decisions or their magnitude, for some people the mere mention of the term decision sends a shiver down their spine.

Every working day, you are faced with the challenge of making decisions. Some of these decisions can have an enormous effect on your day, while others are more mundane:

• Should I complete my adding-value list at the start or end of the day?
• What's the best way to conduct my time audit?
• Which interruption should I work on first?
• Should I go to our weekly meeting or finish my report for the management committee?

Answering these questions is easy for some people because the answers are obvious to them. For others they appear to be more complex. What if they were to get it wrong? Having to make decisions causes anxiety, nervousness and self-doubt. As a result some people find it very difficult to make good decisions.

Indecisive Slaves will cause untold damage to your working day. Hour upon hour will be lost as they ponder endlessly over their decision. They over-analyse and seek too many opinions, which complicates the decision-making process. They worry unduly over whether they can make the correct decision. They are constantly wondering whether or not they have enough information to make the right decision.

'There is no more miserable human being than one in whom nothing is habitual but indecision.'
William James, from *The Principles of Psychology*

Indecisive Slaves fear uncertainty and focus on the potential loss if their decision is wrong. They live by the principle that nobody gets fired for not making a decision, people get fired for making the wrong one. They tend to wait to see if someone will make the decision for them.

How to influence an Indecisive Slave
- Make it easy for them to make a decision by clarifying exactly what they must decide on and what you want to achieve
- Provide options in a logical manner so they can analyse each one carefully and thereby reduce the time needed to make the decision
- Give them all the information required and point them in the direction of where they can receive more information if necessary
- Outline the consequences of making a decision and also the consequences of not making one
- Complete a risk-management analysis for each option
- Agree a course of action and follow up with an action plan with the Indecisive Slave's tasks clearly outlined
- Give them time to make a decision, but set firm deadlines and monitor progress closely

I Want it Now Slaves
I Want it Now Slaves will march to your desk and confidently demand your attention immediately. They strike a commanding posture. They are intense with lots of energy, commitment and drive. They like to make snap decisions and are assured that they are always right. There is a fine line between their confidence and arrogance. They are task-focused and results-driven. A desire to succeed at everything they do often leads to I Want it Now slaves being described as cold, calculating and competitive.

They like people to be honest and frank with them as they are frank and extremely honest with others. They make instant decisions and deal with any fallout at a later time. The main priority for them is to get their tasks completed, even if it means other people's time is taken. Their tasks are always the most important and take a priority over everyone else's.

How to influence an I Want it Now Slave
- Be on time and well prepared for the purpose of your interaction
- Outline what you want from them in an assertive manner
- Be confident and ready for your opinions and position to be challenged robustly

- Ensure you are concise, logical, and avoid waffling at all costs
- Present only the details required for a decision to be made
- Provide a range of solutions so that the I Want it Now Slave can make a choice as soon as possible
- Keep to the agreed agenda and complete on time
- Agree a course of action and follow up with an action plan with the I Want it Now Slave's tasks clearly outlined

Haphazard Slaves

'From nuclear warfare to hand to hand combat, there is only one guiding strategy: target, weapons, movement. If you know what your target is, that will dictate what weapon to use. Once you have your weapon, the weapon will dictate how you move it.' This is the guiding principle to achieving results put forward by ex-Navy SEAL Richard J. Machowicz. Without a clear focus, your results will be inconsistent and unreliable. Time will be wasted thinking about what to do rather than doing what you need to do to get the results. Haphazard Slaves appear to work extremely hard but usually end up at the close of business wondering what they actually achieved. They waste time being busy doing things instead of being busy doing the right things.

'Never confuse motion with action.'
Benjamin Franklin

They feel controlled by their circumstances rather than in control of them; their standards vary greatly depending on mood swings, and there is a lack of self-discipline. Multitasking is a skill that they profess to be one of their strengths when in reality they take on too many tasks. They are great at starting tasks but often fail to finish one before starting another. They try to please everyone, but end up pleasing no one. They often suffer from low self-esteem.

How to influence a Haphazard Slave

- Encourage a Haphazard Slave to focus on one task at a time
- Check to see if they need help or support
- Guide them to where they should use their energy
- Write out clear objectives for them
- Encourage them to focus on solutions rather than dwell on the problems
- Give positive feedback as much as possible
- Celebrate their successes
- Focus their minds on the task at hand
- Enforce deadlines

Let's Have Harmony Slaves

One of the great myths of management is that if employees are happy, then they will work harder and achieve great results. Over the years, organisations have invested heavily in trying to make employees happy, but it doesn't always correlate to higher performance. Let's Have Harmony Slaves also suffer from trying to make everyone happy. They don't like change and are more comfortable in a stable environment.

They are very loyal to the team and their fellow colleagues and are willing to spend a lot of time listening to people's problems and concerns. In return they expect you to spend time listening to them. Let's Have Harmony Slaves have a habit of opening with, 'Sorry to disturb you, but I was wondering if you were free for a minute,' and then they come and sit down in front of you.

Let's Have Harmony Slaves value people and relationships and are very accepting of other people's views. They like to consider all sides of an issue before deciding on the best course of action. They are seen as being non-judgemental.

How to influence a Let's Have Harmony Slave
- Assure them that their opinions are valued
- Give them time to finish tasks
- Allow them to have their say without interrupting them
- Praise them in public and criticise in private
- Demonstrate the benefits of your proposal not only to them but to the rest of the team
- Implement the changes slowly

Leave it 'Til Tomorrow Slaves

'Do you know what happens when you give a procrastinator a good idea? Nothing!' said Donald Gardner. Procrastination is a major cause of wasted time in organisations. Projects are held up, reports are left to the last minute, and stress levels are tested to the limit as you wait patiently on a Leave it 'Til Tomorrow Slave to start the task that you needed done yesterday. Putting off difficult or unpleasant tasks is a common trait for Leave it 'Til Tomorrow Slaves. Unfortunately, most tasks that are put off don't go away – they remain waiting to be done, and they tend to stay at the back of your mind, often causing feelings of guilt and acting as a distraction. More time is wasted thinking about the tasks that have been put off.

Leave it 'Til Tomorrow Slaves appear to be laid-back and easy-going on the outside but can often be in turmoil on the inside. They are easily distracted by people and other, more exciting tasks. They rationalise the fact that the job isn't done by convincing themselves they will start the task first thing tomorrow. They then proceed to carry out various other non-essential tasks and justify this time-wasting by insisting they are making progress. Eventually the deadline will catch up to them and they will pull an all-nighter to finish the task.

How to influence a Leave it 'Til Tomorrow Slave
- Set tasks using the SMARTER Way Goal Setting System™
- Closely monitor their progress
- Break big tasks down into smaller, achievable steps
- Acknowledge their progress by celebrating their success
- Regularly remind them of the reason why they need to complete the tasks
- Understand what motivates them and then use this trigger to keep them focused on the important tasks
- Take corrective action immediately if their progress starts to slow and deadlines begin to slip
- Encourage them at all times
- Make them accountable for their actions

No Plan Slaves
Planning is a waste of time according to some people. As soon as you plan your day you are interrupted and your whole plan is thrown out the window. Some No Plan slaves believe planning is a waste of time because they already know what they have to do on a daily basis. This is a lazy approach to managing your daily activities. It's an easy opt-out excuse. It doesn't take into consideration the non-routine tasks that everyone must deal with.

Planning works because articulating your goals can galvanise your efforts and determination to succeed. Hyrum W. Smith, author of *The Ten Natural Laws of Successful Time and Life Management*, explains that planning is productive as

> a daily planning session can act as a time lever. The cost is small – only ten to fifteen minutes a day – but you will enjoy many benefits all day long, such as clearly defined tasks with deadlines, increased focus on more important tasks, less time spent between projects, and a greater sense of accomplishment at the end of the day.

No Plan Slaves' unstructured approach to work will steal time from you. Their take-it-as-it-comes attitude means they rarely think through the full parameters of the task they need to complete. As a result they don't foresee any potential blockages and may as a consequence underestimate the length of time needed to complete the task on time. This has a knock-on effect for you if you are dependent on their work.

The fact that many will use the excuse that they don't have time to plan is a warning sign they may not be as productive as you need them to be. The much-quoted 'failure to plan is planning to fail' springs to mind yet again. However, No Plan Slaves do like the thrill of the unknown. This unpredictability is their driving force, which needs to be harnessed and controlled to a certain degree. Their cavalier attitude is best epitomised by Sir John Harvey-Jones when he says, 'The nicest thing about not planning is that failure comes as a complete surprise, rather than being preceded by a period of worry and depression.' Ensure that any failures No Plan Slaves encounter are not detrimental to your tasks.

How to influence a No Plan Slave
- Maintain control of all tasks given to No Plan Slaves
- Encourage them to think before they act
- Monitor their progress by continually asking future-based questions, as this will force them to think about what they will do, rather than what they have done
- Keep the plan flexible – No Plan Slaves are often put off by planning, seeing it as being too rigid
- Ask them to identify the blockages they could encounter

Influencing plan

Now that you are familiar with some of techniques available to you, it is time to prepare your influencing plan. You have identified the range of non-value interruptions stealing your time and placed them on the impact/influence grid. In addition to the non-value interruptions, you have also identified who is responsible for them and labelled them according to their slave category.

Write out your proposal for dealing with each non-value interruption. This proposal can include how you will interact with the time-waster, your influencing strategy, the amount of time you will recover, and any potential barriers to your plan. The results will vary depending on each case so it is important to carry out a debriefing session after dealing with each interruption.

Use a scorecard to track each non-value interruption you tackle. This is a great way to give you an 'at a glance' view of which interruptions have been eliminated and how much time you have recovered. It will also track any interruptions that have not been successfully managed and the reason for the failure. Your scorecard will record your position in dealing with non-value interruptions.

Interruption scorecard

Type of interruption	Type of slave	Reason for success/ failure	Time recovered	Date completed

How to say no

Elton John sings a beautiful song entitled 'Sorry Seems to Be the Hardest Word', but for a lot of people, no seems to be the hardest word to say. There are many reasons why people find it difficult to say no: wanting to please everyone, feeling that you are being confrontational if you say no, lack of training in being assertive, and the 'superman effect', which means you take on more than you can handle.

One of the key skills required to be a master of time and to be able to successfully deal with non-value interruptions is your ability to say no. Saying no requires you to be assertive and should not be confused with being aggressive and rude. It is your ability to say what you need to say in a professional, honest and confident manner.

Being assertive comes naturally to some people, while it is a challenge for others. It is important that you are assertive if you are serious about dealing with non-value interruptions as you will need to deal with some difficult time-wasters. The key to being assertive is to follow these simple steps:

- Know what you want and be able to explain it in a clear, confident manner. Practise what you want to say and always practise out loud
- Keep calm and make yourself heard

When was the last time you did this?

You said no to somebody and didn't feel guilty about it.

You took a 30-minute break where you did nothing, had no interruptions and didn't feel guilty about it.

Dos and don'ts of controlling interruptions

Do: Be a master
- Understand you cannot manage time, you must manage yourself and those around you and let time take care of itself
- Take control of dealing with interruptions
- Use the impact/influence grid to achieve large quick-wins
- Develop your influencing skills
- Adapt your influencing style to meet the needs of the person you wish to influence
- Be assertive at all times
- Maintain a scorecard

Don't: Be a slave
- Blame others for your poor use of time
- Fall into the trap of concentrating on the interruptions you have little or no control over
- Ignore the effect that non-value interruptions have on your time
- Use the same strategy to deal with all interruptions
- Be passive when confronted by someone more senior than you who is stealing your time
- Make excuses for not dealing with time-wasting activities

'A vision is not just a picture of what could be; it is an appeal to our better selves, a call to become something more.'
Rosabeth Moss Kanter

'How beautiful it is to do nothing, and then to rest afterward.'
Spanish proverb

- Look the person in the eye and maintain a positive and strong non-verbal position

Saying no to your boss is not easy. However, you need to master this skill, as it can waste a lot of your time if you say yes to all of your boss's demands. The key is not to say no or that you are too busy but to say yes on your terms. Start by asking good, probing questions to confirm in your boss's mind that you are really the best person for the job. If you are, then focus on the level of priority that this task has over your other tasks. Show your boss your full work schedule, which might help you to negotiate a more realistic deadline. This process is not asking your boss to prioritise your work schedule, it is a way of aligning your priorities with his or her needs. Now you are not saying no to the task, but getting agreement on which tasks get done first. Use your adding-value list in your diary to help you deal with your boss's demands.

INTRODUCING MASTER OF TIME TO THE HOME

Time-wasting activities are not confined to the work environment. You face constant interruptions at home. Phone calls, neighbours dropping by, the television, and your inability to say no all steal your time. In the absence of rigid deadlines for many of your home activities, the non-value interruptions are allowed to steal even more time from you because there is no boss monitoring your progress. It is not surprising, then, that so many DIY jobs are left unfinished; the gym membership becomes a costly once-a-year visit, gardens overgrow and hobbies are hit with the procrastination curse. This familiar scenario occurs because of the 'I don't have the time' myth.

Dealing with non-value interruptions is vital if you want to spend your time at home the way you should. The same principles apply. Identify where your time is stolen and then outline your strategy for dealing with these things. Be assertive – your home time is precious. It energises your mind, body and soul. Create a vision of how you would like to spend your time at home and let your vision motivate you to deal with your non-value interruptions.

Before you read any further, take a break and write down the next part of your plan.

PERSONAL THOUGHTS

What will I do differently tomorrow?

MYTH NO. 5
THE BEST WAY TO COMMUNICATE IS
THROUGH MEETINGS

WHAT'S SO GREAT ABOUT MEETINGS?

John liked to arrive early at his desk as he found the 15 minutes before the official start to the day was a good time for him to plan his workload. He had learnt over the years that carefully planning his day had improved his productivity, despite the endless obstacles put in his way by his boss and colleagues. It gave him a structure that appealed to him.

Today was a typical day for John so it came as no surprise that no sooner had the ink dried on his adding-value list than Alex, his boss, called to inform him that she needed to move the team meeting back by 30 minutes because something had cropped up. Another of his carefully thought-out plans now required changing, which wasn't easy. This weekly meeting was always held on Friday, which was the busiest time of the week for John and his colleagues. Unfortunately it suited Alex and she insisted on communicating through team meetings. As the message informing John of the hold-up was being relayed, the first phone call of the day signalled the start of another round of conflicting priorities between attending meetings and the need to deal with phone queries and getting some real work done.

'I'll do it as soon as I get back from our meeting,' John apologetically explained to a frustrated customer who needed an order form urgently. Despite it being the first call of the day, John sounded as if he was already beaten. He was in familiar territory. If only he had no meetings his life

'I have left orders to be awakened at any time in case of national emergency, even if I'm in a cabinet meeting.'

Ronald Reagan

would be so much easier, he lamented as he vaguely listened to the ranting coming from the other end of the phone.

'I'm sorry, but I'm already late,' he said. 'I promise I'll definitely look after it for you as soon as I'm back at my desk. You can trust me, I won't let you down.'

John, now 10 minutes late for the obligatory weekly team meeting, grabbed his jacket, his slightly cold and overly strong coffee, and his work folder, and casually made his way to the board room. On his way he picked up the sales analysis report, which he needed for his next meeting, scheduled for immediately after the team meeting. John usually attended three or four meetings a day, which accounted for between 25 per cent and 60 per cent of his time. Once again, despite being late, he arrived before the meeting had started.

After the usual banter there was an attempt to get the meeting started. There were 12 out of the 15 members of the team present, which was a record high for the team. Usually just over half would be there. Just as the meeting was commencing, right on cue someone would always get an important call and immediately scurry away. John wished he had to courage to slip away too so he could get stuck into his work.

Sipping his coffee, he knew he could just about survive the next 50 or so minutes as Alex, his equally disinterested boss, shared her thoughts and plans for the coming week. Not surprisingly they were the same thoughts, ideas and never-to-be-kept promises that were discussed or, more accurately, voiced last week and the week before. Despite the fact that there had been an agenda circulated the previous day, the topics discussed bore little resemblance to the items listed on the agenda. Nobody ever raised this issue and the meetings often went off on a tangent. There was little two-way communication taking place between Alex and the team. She spoke; they listened.

As usual, John just sat there gazing into his coffee cup as he let his mind wander. He had surrendered to yet another unproductive meeting. He spent much of the meeting thinking about the pile of work on his desk and the number of e-mails he would have to read when he eventually made it back – staying awake was a challenge. Essentially it was a sales report outlining what was done (or should have been done) the previous week. Each sales rep took it in turn to list their sales completions and give their excuses on why they were failing to meet their targets. John could never see the point of this exercise because if they

'The trouble with being punctual is that nobody's there to appreciate it.'
Franklin P. Jones

'When there is something to be said, it is better if it is said right away. If it is said later, it will sound like an excuse.'
Yamamoto Tsunetomo,
The Book of the Samurai

were behind in their sales figures, wouldn't it be more beneficial to be out there looking for more business?

Although this meeting was scheduled to last 60 minutes (and often ran longer), there was only about 10 minutes of information that directly impacted on John. Out of these 10 minutes, only two minutes directly impacted on the other members of the team. So, out of the hour the meeting lasted, only two minutes of discussion were relevant to both John and his colleagues.

Two-and-a-half hours, five cups of coffee, twelve additional tasks and a thumping headache later, John somewhat less than ecstatically returned to his desk, which was now covered in messages. Another morning wasted with badly planned meetings. His organisation's obsession with meetings was slowing strangling him. He felt many of these meetings were called because of habit or fear that the place would collapse if people didn't have them. It seemed the only way people could communicate with management was through meetings. It would take someone with vision and courage to put a halt to this time-wasting activity. Research carried out by Dr Margaret Burn found that less than 15 per cent of meetings achieved the objectives set for the meeting by the group.

What is a meeting?

Over time, some words take on a negative meaning contrary to their original meaning. For instance, bureaucracy is associated with endless forms, a way of making life difficult for people, something to be avoided at all costs. Meetings are fast becoming a byword for inefficiency. People now bemoan the trend to have endless meetings. It seems that this is the only way to communicate. People now regularly have meetings about meetings. The *Collins Dictionary* gives two definitions for the word meeting: (1) coming together, encounter, confrontation, engagement, rendezvous; (2) assembly, conference, convention, get-together, gathering.

The second definition is straightforward in so far that it states what a meeting is – a gathering of people. The first definition is more interesting as it explains some of the key components of a meeting. It defines what the real purpose of a meeting is – the coming together of people with opinions, views and something to offer the rest of the attendees. There should be engagement of all attendees and confrontation should be welcomed and managed properly. This broad definition views meetings as a positive use of your time. What follows is an examination of

When was the last time you did this?

You attended a meeting that was boring, badly run, non-informative, ran over time, had no agenda, and was a waste of your time. How often does this happen, and how much time do you waste attending such meetings?

why so many meetings fail, particularly team or group ones, and how masters of time avoid the pitfalls of badly organised meetings.

Is there a need for so many people at meetings?

Bill Gates tackled the subject of having too many meetings in his book *Business @ the Speed of Thought*:

> The manager asked one question – a common question at Microsoft I like to ask – 'Why are there so many people in this room?' In any meeting I want only the essential decision makers. Everybody else should be off solving other problems. If you find more than three or four decision makers in the room, you can be sure that the sheer number of people involved is a major part of the problem.

Too many decision makers often leads to paralysis through analysis and the fact that everyone wants to speak. Egos take over and everyone believes that if they are present at a meeting, then they should air their views. There is more talking than listening, and as a consequence very few decisions are made. Add in any office politics and the amount of time wasted is substantially increased. This slave-like behaviour is present in organisations because very few people ever lose their jobs for not making a decision; the brave ones who do make a decision that subsequently turns out to be wrong are the ones who get the sack. As a result, many organisations inadvertently promote time-wasting activities in meetings.

Meetings for the sake of meetings

Team meetings have become a major vehicle for slave-like behaviour. The consequences are costly for both organisations and its people. Such slave-like behaviours include allowing meetings to start late, run over their allotted time, discuss issues not relevant to all the attendees and are held out of habit. Meetings are often held with no real purpose except to communicate some report or findings, which could be achieved through other, more efficient methods. Most team meetings are set up to fail because of lack of preparation time, poor facilitation skills and apathy.

Despite the criticisms thrown at meetings they are still widely used. Some slaves to the clock could attend three or more meetings a day. This could easily represent between 50 per cent and 80 per cent of their day. Scott Snair wrote in *Stop the Meeting I Want to Get Off* that

Holding meetings, at some point, becomes as natural as breathing. And the suggestion that these daily sessions are unproductive or bad for business doesn't register because there simply doesn't seem to be an alternative way of doing things.

Invest your time wisely

It may be true that it is hard to find an alternative solution to meetings, but it doesn't mean you can't search for a better way of communicating or that you cannot improve the way you use meetings. If holding meetings is the way you conduct your business and you aren't convinced there is an alternative, try out the following steps before you attend your next meeting.

Step 1: Should this meeting be held?

Holding meetings has become a staple in the corporate world. Some companies will have daily, weekly and monthly team meetings to continually update staff on their performance and what is happening within their organisation. On the surface, keeping staff informed continually seems like a good use of time.

However, before you organise your next team meeting, ask yourself some straightforward questions to help you decide if this is the best use of everyone's time:

- Does your staff need a team meeting to tell them how they are performing?
- Is there a better way of communicating your message?
- What is the real purpose of your meeting?
- Should these meetings be held?

As well as face-to-face meetings, some organisations are hooked on their video-conferencing facilities and will include as many people as possible in this type of meeting, simply because technology will allow them to do so. Managers sometimes have the impression that this method of communicating is saving time. Initially this was the case as it saved on travel time. Now, however, because they are so easy to set up, people are using video-conferencing to have more and more meetings. The time saved on travelling has been counterbalanced by an increase in the number of meetings scheduled this way.

While meetings are useful for sharing ideas and information, making key decisions and tracking progress on projects, you must ask yourself if all meetings are, in fact, necessary. Glenn Parker and Robert Hoffman ask this question in the opening chapter of their book, *Meeting Excellence*: 'Yet sometimes, deciding not to meet may be the best use of everyone's valuable time.' Like most habits, this one can be hard to break. Masters of time invest their time wisely when it comes to attending and holding meetings. They only hold meetings that add value to the attendees.

Step 2: Should you attend this meeting?

When you complete your time audit you will discover the true cost attending meetings has on your time. This will include the travel time, preparation for the meeting and additional tasks that are added to your list as a result of attending each meeting. You should also note the times these meetings were scheduled for and whether they were suitable or interrupted the most productive part of your day.

Before you attend your next meeting, ask yourself the following two key questions:

- What will I contribute to this meeting?
- What will I get from this meeting?

If the answers are 'nothing', you should seriously consider if attending this meeting is the best use of your time. Plan your exit strategy. Send someone else who would answer positively to at least one of those questions. Alternatively, confront the meeting organiser and ask to be excluded from the meeting. State your reasons in a positive way. If your presence is required purely for informational purposes, get a copy of the report instead. Avoid wasting time by not attending non-essential meetings.

Step 3: Preparation for the meeting

Step 1 establishes if a meeting is meaningful and a good use of time, while Step 2 examines if it is appropriate for you to attend. Assuming that the meeting is meaningful and you are the best person to attend, you need to prepare properly to ensure you invest your time profitably. There are three types of meetings you need to prepare for:

Informational. These are meetings where someone is passing on some beneficial information to you. Try to get as much documentation as you can prior to the meeting so you can plan your questions. Prepare to take key notes so that you can refer to them later or pass them on to other members of the team. Long, informational meetings tend to lose focus, so ensure you are ready to engage in active listening, otherwise you run the risk of daydreaming during the session, particularly if the presenter is not engaging.

Discussion. This type of meeting requires a lot of participation. Research the subject matter beforehand. Establish what knowledge or expertise the other attendees expect you to bring to the meeting. Keep your materials concise and relevant to the topic. There is a tendency for this type of meeting to run over and go around in circles. Think of ways you can keep everyone focused on the subject matter. Determine the time the meeting is scheduled to finish and inform everyone that you must leave at that time. Do not allow over-runs to occur.

Decisional. The purpose here is that there is a decision made during the meeting. Only invite the key decision makers and keep the group small. Agree a framework for decision-making and keep to it. Get a copy of all the relevant information prior to the meeting and brief yourself fully. After each decision is made, review the process to establish if it is working in a productive and time-efficient manner. Critically, for masters of time, they determine if the decision-making process is adding real value to them and their organisation.

Meeting audit

A carefully planned meeting audit will act as a catalyst for a radical rethink on the need for meetings as it will highlight the real issues that contribute to non-value meetings. The results of your audit will provide you with a framework to build an action plan to rid yourself of any slave-like behaviours. It will help you to continue with the productive meetings and eliminate the time-wasting activities of the non-productive meetings.

Apart from the distractions and interruptions that team meetings often cause, they eat up a lot of valuable time for staff who greatly require that time to finish key tasks. Therefore it is good management practice to carry out audits on meetings on a regular basis. They will confirm how many hours you are spending preparing, organising and attending meetings, and determine if this is the best use of your time.

Step 1: Establish if the meeting still serves a purpose

Are your meetings held out of habit, because no one had the courage to stop them, or do they serve a real purpose? Barbara J. Streibel, author of

> **When was the last time you did this?**
>
> Conduct a meeting audit to establish how many hours you spend preparing and attending meetings and if it is the best use of your time.

Plan and Conduct Effective Meetings – 24 Steps to Generate Meaningful Results, says, 'If you don't have a purpose, don't hold a meeting.' Before you begin to plan your next meeting, ask yourself two simple questions that will save you time:

- Why do you need to hold this meeting?
- What tangible results will be achieved at the meeting that will add value to you and your fellow attendees?

The answer to the first question will outline the key reason why the meeting is important and should take place. Clearly state this reason on the agenda as a purpose statement and then determine afterwards if all attendees' objectives were met. Your purpose statement should be reviewed every time you call a meeting so that the reason for meeting is still relevant.

The second answer will help to ensure no one's time is wasted as you will have a specific list to determine the success factors of the meeting. These are the results that can be evaluated and implemented. It is also worth establishing if the purpose of the meeting can be achieved in a more time-efficient manner.

Step 2: Establish the true cost of the meeting and carry out a cost/ benefit analysis

Meetings are a cost to you and should be subjected to a regular cost/ benefit analysis. They use up time whether they are productive or non-productive. Barbara J. Streibel asks, 'What are the costs in time and energy, in morale, in work attitude, in the impact on you and your career? What are the benefits?' These questions need answers to determine the true cost of any slave-like behaviours associated with meetings.

Start by listing the number of meetings that impact on you on a daily, weekly and monthly basis. Calculate the amount of time they take up, including preparation and travel time. It is worth remembering that all time has a value – there is no such thing as free time. Eugene Griessman explains:

> To make that point, a CEO of a large corporation brought a 'money clock' into the executive meeting room. Attendees of the meeting punched in. The clock, which was programmed with the hourly rate of each attendee, calculated the amount of time that was elapsing and the total cost of the meeting in dollars. The CEO made his point. Meetings that run on and on seem to be free, but they can be extremely costly.

What would be the hourly cost of a meeting with 12 attendees? If you take the average rate per hour for the attendees to be €35 then a simple calculation would be:

- 12 attendees at €35 per hour = €420 per hour for each meeting
- 3 one-hour team meetings per day = 3 x €420 = €1,260
- 15 per week = 15 x €420 = €6,300
- 780 per year = 780 x €420 = €327,600

This calculation is the straightforward payroll cost for the duration of the meeting itself for 12 people, but a fairer reflection on costs must take into consideration the preparation time, the travelling time to and from the meeting, the socialising time that accompanies meetings, and the loss of productivity time. If you take this calculation these further steps and calculate the payroll costs over a year you start to get a feel for the real costs of meetings in monetary terms.

Once the costs are calculated you then need to find out if the output of the meetings are contributing real value to you, your organisation or the attendees. A full analysis can be carried out at this point to evaluate which meetings are affordable. Loss-making meetings should be reviewed before more are called.

Step 3: Establish who should attend the meeting and what their contribution will be

Now that you know the real cost of a meeting you can decide who should attend. There are two simple questions that must be answered on behalf of all potential attendees.

- What will the attendee get from the meeting?
- What will the attendee contribute to the meeting?

Put an end to the slave-like behaviour of inviting as many people as possible to meetings just because they have a vague connection to the subject matter or that they attended a previous meeting. Save people's time by only issuing invitations to those needed to achieve the purpose and desired outcomes of the meeting.

Step 4: Has the meeting become stale, routine, or a one-way communication tool?

All meetings have a life cycle. Some start out as a breath of fresh air; attendees are enthused, ideas are discussed robustly and decisions are made that add great value to all. Over time they can begin to lose their effectiveness and become stale. They become a waste of everyone's time.

Therefore it's essential that you, as an attendee, watch out for some of the indicators that signal your meeting is moving rapidly towards its sell-by date. Some of the warning signs include:

- Key people failing to turn up
- Speakers wandering off on tangents
- Action plans are not followed up on
- Concentration levels are lowered
- Mobile phone calls are taken
- General lack of focus
- Little or no discussion takes place
- Meetings are cancelled at the last minute for trivial reasons

If you attend a meeting that has become stale or fails regularly to accomplish its purpose then you must decide to either radically overhaul it or make it redundant by opting out. Explain to the organiser that you believe it no longer serves its purpose.

Step 5: Is the timing of when the meeting takes place correct?
A key issue for managing your use of time is the actual start time of meetings. A thorough audit will find out if:

- Meetings are scheduled for a busy part of the day
- The time is suitable for all attendees and not just the chief organiser
- Meetings overlap for some attendees

Get the scheduling wrong and the attendees won't have their minds fully focused on the meeting's objectives. They will be concentrating on the tasks left on their desk or what they need for the next meeting. This is a typical problem with the logistics of arranging meetings, which results in a serious waste of time for some attendees.

Step 6: Is there a better alternative?
Can you achieve the purpose and outcomes of your meeting through a phone call, memo, teleconferencing, or e-mail? Each of these options has benefits and should be explored to assess its feasibility. Evaluate each method to see if there is an alternative way to achieve the same results your meeting accomplishes in a quicker timeframe.

An effective audit will improve the overall performance of your meetings, both the meetings you organise and the ones you attend. At the heart of a good audit is its ability to highlight key areas where time is lost, identify areas where your time could be put to better use and help to achieve the main purpose of your meetings. Adopt a holistic approach to your findings instead of focusing in on one point. Put your results into perspective by assessing the risks of doing something verses doing nothing. Then decide on the action required to make your meetings more useful, and implement your decision.

Agendas for successful meetings

Effective meetings don't happen by chance or luck. They are the product of good planning, the ability to organise and control. Sir Adrian Cadbury writes in his book *The Company Chairman* that 'setting the agenda is one of the ways in which the chairman exercises control over the meeting. It is important that the matters to be discussed at a board meeting are signalled by the agenda.' Whether it is a formal board meeting or weekly team meeting, it is imperative you control it, otherwise time will be lost.

As the organiser of the meeting you need to control who should attend, what the purpose is, what you want to achieve, where it will take place and also how much time it will consume. It is your responsibility to ensure that no one's time is wasted. Your agenda will play a vital role in controlling how the time is spent during the meeting.

A good agenda, as outlined earlier, begins with the purpose statement. This informs everyone why it is being held and what you want to achieve. It is a focused introduction to the meeting and also helps people to decide if they should attend, or decline your invitation. Next you should outline the topics you wish to cover and label them as informational, decisional or discussion. This labelling indicates the level of participation required from all attendees. Prioritise your topics and always begin the meeting with a topic that will engage all the attendees. The next stage is to assign a timeframe to each topic. This is critical if you wish to manage the length of time the meeting will take up. Keep the meeting as brief as possible. Allan Leighton, one of Britain's top business leaders, believes that 'the first 20 minutes of a meeting are its most productive part'.

The last topic on the agenda should be a wrap-up session. This session should find out how good the meeting was. Did it achieve its objective? How was the time used? Did it stay on track? Were all topics covered? The information gathered in these final few minutes will enhance future meetings.

The agenda is circulated to all attendees, together with any research materials or reports. This will reduce the amount of time spent on the preparation. Also enclose a copy of the rules of engagement, which will highlight the start and finish times and the consequences of breaking any of the rules.

I don't like meetings

Today, meetings suffer from a poor image. Research shows that 50 per cent of managers believe meetings are a total waste of their time. They annoy and demoralise many workers. Scott Snair, author of *Stop the Meeting I Want to Get Off*, explored the reasons so many people dislike meetings, and found that time was a big factor.

> First, meetings take time – and lots and lots of it. The time consumed is rarely well scheduled or well managed. Management studies suggest that about half of all time spent in a meeting is unproductive – and I would label those studies as generous. When you are at a meeting, even one that you have convened, your most valuable resource – time – is being used up.

The amount of time you spend attending meetings adds up to a lot of time wasted in an already full workload. An article by Susan Bowles in *USA Today* states that 'According to a 20-year study, Minnesota professor Roger K. Mosvick found average employees spend 8½ hours a week in meetings. Middle managers spend 10½ hours, and top executives spend 12.'

Other factors that give meetings a bad name include badly managed meetings that start late and run over time. No agendas are produced and, as a consequence, lengthy discussions are allowed when side issues overshadow important topics. Lack of control by the chair means no one takes responsibility to get the meeting back on track.

Slaves to the clock attend every meeting they are invited to and precious time is wasted. They attend because they are afraid they may miss out on something, they are afraid to say no, they fail to prepare properly by reading the agenda and most of all they fail to see how much time they waste by attending non-productive meetings. Slaves to the clock will be in the middle of completing an important and urgent task when they will suddenly stop and go to an unimportant meeting. Often the attraction is the informal socialising that accompanies non-productive meetings, such as bringing food and coffee to the meeting and hanging around afterwards appearing to engage in work-related conversation. This behaviour causes stress and missed deadlines.

By contrast, a master of time will look at ways to minimise the number of meetings they attend. Robert E. Kelly explains in his book *How to Be a Star at Work* the strategies star performers use to get the most out of their day. He says, 'Many try to build meeting-free days into their weekly schedules to give themselves periods of concentration time.' Unless the meeting adds value, you must be assertive and say no.

INTRODUCING MASTER OF TIME TO THE HOME

When you arrive home after a hard day managing endless meetings you would think the dreaded meeting monster is left behind. It is your chance to have a few meeting-free hours when you can recharge your batteries. Unfortunately the curse of meetings has followed you home: the parent/teacher meeting, the football committee meeting, the residence association meeting, the meeting for those who are addicted to meetings meeting and, because people's lives are so busy, there are now family meetings.

If 50 per cent of your meetings in work are a waste of time, can you imagine how much time is wasted in 'home' meetings? Your time at home is precious and, if you feel the need to call a family meeting in order to talk to all of your family, it is time to conduct a meeting audit for home. Family time should not be scheduled to fit in-between wasteful activities. It should be fun and spontaneous. Ruthlessly eliminate any meeting that wastes your time and spend this time with your family and friends doing the things that add value to your life.

Before you read any further, take a break and write down the next part of your plan.

Dos and don'ts of meetings

Do: Be a master
- Conduct a meeting audit
- Find alternative options to team meetings
- Have an agenda for a meeting
- Write meeting purpose statements
- Continually ask the two critical questions:

  What will I contribute to this meeting?
  What will I get from this meeting?

- Try to plan a meeting-free day

Don't: Be a slave
- Attend meetings out of habit
- Daydream at meetings
- Allow meetings to start late
- Fail to participate
- Waste time bringing drinks and food to meetings
- Allow non-productive meetings to interrupt important tasks

PERSONAL THOUGHTS

What will I do differently tomorrow?

MYTH NO. 6
IT'S QUICKER IF I DO IT MYSELF

DELEGATION: PRINCIPLES OF EFFECTIVE ORGANISING

John is swamped with work. It's that time again when the monthly sales figures are due. His stress levels are building as the 3:00 deadline approaches. All around him, his colleagues are busy working, but none are helping him with the sales figures. They seem oblivious to his plight. Could there be a task more pressing at this moment? John keeps his head down and continues his solo fight against the monthly deadline. Every time he hears his boss Alex's voice he buries his head further, hoping she won't see him. Although he knows he'll have to face her eventually, he isn't ready for his failures to be exposed to the rest of his team just yet. That embarrassment can wait, but the sales figures can't.

'Do you need a hand with those reports, John?' Craig, the newest member of the team, finally asks.

'No, Craig, thanks for asking but it's quicker if I do it myself,' John replies politely, but with a bluntness that surprises Craig.

Craig is very enthusiastic and willing to learn new tasks. But, much to his annoyance, he regularly has his offer of assistance turned down by John and other senior colleagues for the reason, 'It's quicker if I do it myself.' This assertion puzzles Craig as it's clearly quicker if there's an additional pair of hands helping. It's no wonder, then, that John gets little help from anyone on his team, as he's very unwilling to pass on any of his tasks to his colleagues. He simply refuses to delegate.

Is it really quicker for John to do it himself? He is keen to perform well, but his insistence on being a martyr is his downfall. His current workload makes it impossible for him to achieve his deadlines without help from someone. Working harder and longer is clearly getting him nowhere, as he regularly misses key deadlines. He is under increasing pressure so it is harder for him to trust someone else with getting the tasks done right. He is not managing himself or his colleagues very well.

His reluctance to take up the offer of assistance from his colleagues may seem like bizarre behaviour. But is John alone? Slaves to the clock are classic martyrs. They will try, and often fail, to do everything themselves. They feel they should be able to complete their workload and that passing on work could be seen as being unable to cope with their job. Have you ever used the short-sighted phrase, 'It's quicker if I do it myself'?

On closer examination, this theory is an exercise in false economy for John. Initially it would appear that to show Craig how to do the report would take more time than if John was to do it himself. However, if he had invested some time in developing Craig and others, he would reap the rewards over the weeks and months that follow. Slaves to the clock like John are penny wise and pound foolish. They fail to see the benefits that delegating brings to their time management strategy. They are trapped in a fire-fighting mentality.

John needs to move from being exclusively a doer to being a manager of people. He needs to see people as a resource to be utilised as often as possible. If he learned a few simple steps of delegating, not only would he improve how he manages his time, but he would also improve as a manager and colleague.

Is it quicker to do it yourself?

Slaves to the 'it's quicker if I do it myself' school of thought fail to see how much time is wasted every day by this misguided notion. It is a warning sign that they are spending too much time fire-fighting and not enough time being strategically focused. There is a lack of planning of their daily tasks. Their head is buried in the job instead of every so often taking a step back, lifting their head up and looking beyond their current task. They need to ask themselves a simple question, 'Is it the best use of my time to be doing the tasks that I'm currently working on?'

If you can relate to this, one way forward is to list all of your daily tasks and jobs. You have all the information you need in your time audit report. Review the list and highlight any task that could be performed by someone other than you. There are a few other key points that should be answered by your analysis.

How much time do these jobs take up? Your audit will give you the exact time, including interruptions, which each task took during the review period. Write this figure beside each task on your list – it will be useful later when deciding which tasks would be beneficial to delegate. If you have listed a task not in your time audit, place an estimated time against it.

Are these jobs adding value to you and your career? Score each task/ job you currently perform by deciding if it adds value in any way to you and your career, or if the task/job adds no value. Although this exercise is subjective, it produces a snapshot of the tasks that are important to you and those tasks that should be delegated, if possible, because they are non-value tasks. You will also highlight through this exercise how much time you waste doing non-value tasks.

How many of these tasks are 'hobby jobs' that you like doing? 'Hobby jobs' can be very hard to let go. They are the tasks you enjoy performing but should be done by someone else. Highlight these tasks to ensure they are dealt with appropriately.

What could you do with the excess time? If you weren't doing the tasks you are going to delegate, what would you replace them with? It should go without saying that each delegated task should be replaced by a task that will add real value to you, your organisation and your career. Carefully choose these tasks, preferably from your Green Priority C time (important but not urgent tasks).

Who could do these tasks for you? Develop a list of suitable colleagues who you can call upon when you have a task available to delegate. Write out a profile for each person. Their profile is a detailed description of their level of knowledge, skills and expertise. Build up their profile over a period of time with the information you gather from debriefing sessions you carry out after a delegated task is completed. (This is discussed in more detail later in this chapter.) This is an ongoing process.

Who would benefit by doing these jobs? Once you have developed a list of suitable candidates for delegation you should prioritise them based on the benefits each one will gain from the selected tasks. You should also carry out a time/benefit analysis to ensure you will recover enough time to make the delegation process beneficial to you.

If you continue doing these tasks, will you have enough time left to do the things that really matter to you? The best way to get a sense of why you should delegate as much as possible is to establish the consequences of not delegating.

Answering the above questions will give you a clear understanding of whether you are spending your time wisely or if you are simply being busy doing tasks. You will probably find that there are a number of jobs you are currently doing that would serve you better if you passed them on to someone else. Some of these tasks can easily be delegated, while others require more thought and planning.

Impact/influence grid

Using the impact/influence grid will help you to organise the tasks you can delegate based on their complexity and time saved. You first used this matrix to give yourself a snapshot of your time-wasting activities and it allowed you to see very quickly where your focus should be in order to improve your productivity. The key to its success was using the matrix to tackle the high-impact and high-influence interruptions first before expending any energy on dealing with high-impact, low-influence activities.

The same principles can apply to delegating. Seek out the tasks that can be easily passed on to someone else and start the process of delegating with them. Achieve some quick and easy wins early so that you can begin to reap the rewards as quickly as possible. Taking time to involve people in the delegation process will ensure a big payoff. Because of their involvement, they will understand the reasons you are delegating tasks to them and also the benefits they will obtain from the delegation process. Over a period of time you could delegate up to 25 per cent of your routine tasks. How much time would that recover for you? The impact/influence grid is an ideal format to give a snapshot of the best approach to take with your delegation strategy.

Impact/influence grid

A Action now	B Be ruthless
C Can you influence?	D Don't waste any more time

Tasks that are in **Quadrant A** should be delegated immediately as they have a high impact on your time and you can easily influence others to do them for you. They are the routine jobs you have identified that can be competently completed by other people who have the necessary skills and are eager to do them.

Quadrant B tasks require you to be ruthless and to delegate frequently as, although they don't take too much of your time, they are tasks that require little effort in delegating. They may consist of some of your 'hobby jobs' or tasks you are reluctant to let go of.

Quadrant C tasks are more complex and time-consuming. Initially they would appear to justify the myth of, 'It's quicker if I do it myself.' However, if you invest a little time in planning your delegation strategy for these tasks, the rewards will be worth it as they consume of lot of your time. Your colleagues may not have the skills to complete these tasks at first, but with some training and guidance they will develop them. Quadrant C tasks are tasks that slaves to the clock fail to manage.

Quadrant D tasks are the jobs you are probably better off completing yourself. These are the tasks that would take more time to explain to someone than doing yourself. They are generally short, complex, one-off activities that require a lot of skill or knowledge to perform. Don't waste any time trying to delegate these tasks.

The 'it's quicker if I do it myself' myth can be overcome through investing time in planning your work schedule and developing your delegating skills. *Door to Door* is an award-winning film about the life of Bill Porter, who was a door-to-door salesman who overcame the challenges of cerebral palsy to become salesman of the year for his company. Although he was told that he was unemployable, he never allowed his pain or people's biases to stop him from being successful in his long career. This was also due in part to his mother's unwavering support and two characteristics she instilled in Bill: patience and perseverance. Developing your delegation skills will require both of these characteristics. There may be a lot of pain and resistance initially, but your effort over time will yield real success. Using the impact/influence grid will give you a clear picture of the different strategies needed to delegate your selected tasks.

'Nothing is impossible if you can delegate.'

The benefits of delegation are wide-ranging and include the following:

- Frees up your time from routine work to enable you to complete value-adding tasks
- Reduces personal job overload
- Increases the job satisfaction of the delegate, who now has more responsibility and variety in their work
- Improves your capacity and the delegate's capabilities
- Assists with your career planning and development
- Gives you more time to plot your future career path and remain competitive
- Gets you out of the office on time

What is delegation?

One of the characteristics of slaves to the clock is their reluctance to delegate. Their reasons are many and varied and will be discussed later in this chapter. However, to gain from the benefits of delegation it is important to understand what is meant by the term. It is a common word used by both managers and staff in every type of business, but few people understand its full meaning and, more importantly, how to manage delegation as a means of improving their use of time.

Delegation of authority is the process whereby you give a colleague part of your own authority to make decisions, which in turn will get the job done by someone other than you. Overall responsibility for the completion of the task, however, cannot be delegated. If you choose an inept person to do a task, it's still your fault if it goes wrong and you cannot escape blame by pointing the finger elsewhere. Robert Heller, author of *How to Delegate*, says, 'Delegating involves entrusting another person with a task for which the delegator remains ultimately responsible.'

Delegation is universally recognised as an important skill in managing people. It requires knowledge, time, trust and courage. Failure can be extremely costly for all concerned. Masters of time use their delegation skills often and wisely in order to free up their time. They overcome the constraints of time by passing a range of routine and non-value tasks on to others who could do them just as easily and competently. Masters of time use delegation as a tool to manage themselves, which in turn helps them to manage how they use their time.

Delegation, if properly done, is not an abdication of duties or the dumping of boring tasks on to other staff, but an important managerial skill. It is not about getting rid of tasks you find boring or think are beneath you. It is the art of managing your workload rather than simply doing the work.

Trust–control dilemma

Control + Trust = Constant

The trust-control dilemma revolves around the fact that the tighter the control you exercise over a task, the lower the level of trust between you and the delegate. By improving your delegation skills, you can build trust and thereby loosen your control. Trust can be built by improving the skills of the delegate, reviewing the tasks that were completed, and by constant feedback between you.

Obstacles to delegation

Delegation recovers time better spent adding real value to you and your organisation. It allows you to focus on important tasks. However, despite the many benefits delegation provides, people still find it hard to delegate. Successful delegation requires a high level of skill, effective support and a resolution of the trust-control dilemma. As a result, many people are reluctant to delegate and attempt to handle their many routine matters themselves in addition to their complex tasks. This can be due to a number of factors, including:

- You can't find the time to delegate
- You perceive your job as a solo activity
- You like to give the impression of being overworked
- You fear being replaced by junior staff, or delegating yourself out of a job
- You are unable or unwilling to let go of your tasks
- You want to keep control
- You are not trained in delegating skills and fail to see how it improves your your time
- You have a low opinion of your colleagues and therefore have low confidence and trust in their abilities to get the job done
- No one is willing to take on the delegated task

Each of these reasons can be overcome by developing a robust step-by-step delegating process. This systematic approach will initially require an investment of your time, but the rewards will be significant. It will help to eliminate the following excuses that people often use to avoid delegating:

- 'It takes too long to explain.'
- 'If you want a job done right then you have to do it yourself.'
- 'It's too complicated to explain and I'm the only one that really knows how to do it correctly.'

If you use any of these excuses, it is likely costing you endless hours doing tasks other people should be doing. Use the following process to reduce this wastage and gain the time benefits that delegation offers you.

Delegation, step by step

Developing a process for delegating will increase your chances for successfully passing tasks on to other people, which ultimately reduces the

When was the last time you did this?
Freed up some valuable time by delegating a key task to a colleague and the task was completed to the standard agreed.

amount of wasted time. By concentrating on the process you can easily adapt it to suit each task you have identified as being suitable to delegate to a colleague. Professional golfer Padraig Harrington believes that if 'you get the process right then success will follow'. Successful delegation requires that people have the right skills and the authority to do the job, and are given feedback on their performance. To ensure consistency in delegation, you need to follow a systematic approach that involves a number of steps.

Step 1	Identify the parameters of the task to be delegated
Step 2	Identify a suitable colleague for delegation
Step 3	Brief the delegate and gain task acceptance
Step 4	Provide support to the delegate
Step 5	Control task performance
Step 6	Debrief the delegate

Step 1: Identify the parameters of the task to be delegated

The process begins with identifying the tasks you are going to delegate. Review your time-audit log and determine which tasks are not adding value to you. You need to analyse the benefits of delegating these tasks, including the time you will free up versus the time you will invest in the process. Once you have established the best tasks to delegate, you then proceed to defining the full parameters of these tasks. This is a crucial stage which, if overlooked, can cause you to lose a lot of time later because of mistakes and omissions.

Defining the parameters of the tasks includes being able to describe in detail what needs to done, the standard the task must be completed to, the length of time it will take and the level of knowledge and skill required to successfully complete the chosen task. This may appear obvious, but it is the source of much wasted time as both parties engage in assumptions. The delegator assumes they have explained the task fully and the delegate assumes they have the required information to complete the task. Often it is only on completion of the task that both parties actually communicate properly.

It is good practice to write out the parameters of each task in a briefing document, as you will find out whether or not you have all the relevant information about the task. Label each task. Highlight the various milestones that will help you to monitor the progress of the task. Use this in Step 5 to set up your control system. Also, you can use this briefing document again when you need to delegate this task to someone else.

Step 2: Identify a suitable colleague for delegation

The second step in the process is determining the most suitable person for the selected task to be delegated to. This involves establishing if the person has completed the task previously and, if so, whether the results were satisfactory. If they are new to the task, the key question that needs to be answered is: do they have the necessary skills, knowledge and expertise to complete the task? Another important factor is to establish their attitude towards taking on additional work. Will they be positive and enthusiastic about completing the task, or will there be resistance?

Max Landsberg's skill/will matrix is designed to help you establish the level of skill and the attitude of the person you wish to delegate to. It is a snapshot of their current position and helps you to decide on the best course of action to take when delegating to them. It ensures that you don't delegate inappropriately by giving tasks to people who are either unable or unwilling to complete them. This is a common mistake made by those who delegate without using a good process. Alternatively, you can be too hands-on with someone who is both willing and capable of doing the job without your help. Closely monitoring these people will only frustrate you both and lead to conflict.

> 'The secret of success is not in doing your own work but in recognising the right man to do it.'
> Andrew Carnegie

Skill/will matrix

B **Educate** High will Low skill	A **Delegate** High will High skill
C **Motivate and educate** Low will Low skill	D **Motivate** Low will High skill

Adapted from Max Landsberg's skill/will matrix.

Quadrant A is where your delegate is both willing and able to do the tasks. They are experienced and are eager to develop themselves by taking on additional tasks. This is the place you need to position your colleagues if delegation is to be straightforward and successful. No matter which quadrant you place a delegate into initially, you need to move them into this quadrant to delegate effectively and with minimum time lost.

Ensure that you provide the freedom to do the job for Quadrant A people. Give them the scope of the task and encourage them to take responsibility for the method. Use questions like: 'What do you think is the best approach to take with this task?', 'What level of support do you need from me?' and, 'How will this task benefit you?' Remember to offer praise and support while they are performing the task.

Quadrant B is where the will is high, but the skill level is low. It is likely that people in this quadrant are enthusiastic newcomers who are willing to learn new tasks. It is important to harness this willingness by investing time in training. As soon as you move them from Quadrant B to Quadrant A, you can delegate the task to them. Be careful not to confuse their enthusiasm to take on the task with their ability to do the task. Get the sequence right – educate first and then delegate – so you won't waste time correcting mistakes later.

Quadrant C is the challenging area. This is where both the skill and will is low. People in this component could be there because they are new to the job. They could be afraid to try out new tasks as a result of previous bad experiences. They could be resistant to change in general. This is also where a lot of time can be wasted through focusing on developing the person's skills and ignoring their lack of willingness to do the task. The mistake is assuming that if they knew how to do the task then they would suddenly be willing to do it. The sequence of events is crucial in order to maximise your investment of time in dealing with people in Quadrant C. First, you need to build their will, and then the skill, before you move them to Quadrant A where you then delegate.

Build their will by spending time on developing the relationship between you. Establish their core motivational drivers by asking good, open questions. Link their motivational drivers to the reason why they should undertake the tasks you wish to delegate to them. Continually encourage and nurture with constructive feedback when they perform the tasks and finish on a high with a strong debriefing session. As soon as they are motivated and ready for their new tasks, then you can start to educate. Bring some structure to the tasks and then start the training, which will fill in any skill gaps. This sequence makes the whole process easier as the delegate is no longer resisting new challenges.

Quadrant D is where the skills are there but the will is low. This component can be tricky to deal with because the people are highly experienced and skilled but lack motivation. There can any number of reasons why motivation is low. There could be personal issues; your style of delegating might be conflicting with their style of working; or they simply may be overloaded with tasks already. Remember some of your most highly motivated colleagues may fall into this quadrant occasionally.

The key to managing people in this quadrant is to invest your time in building their will. Focus on their desire to achieve, look at incentives that might help, check their confidence level and show a lot of interest. Bring excitement back into the tasks. Using the SMARTER Way Goal Setting System™ will help you here.

When you apply the skill/will matrix it will ensure that, whoever you choose, you are taking the appropriate approach with them when you delegate. It helps you to decide on your strategy and whether you need to focus on motivating, or educating, or both. This saves time when it comes to the next step, which is your briefing session.

Before you move on to Step 3 there is another factor to take into consideration when choosing your candidate for delegating. That is to identify their personality type. This will be helpful when you plan your briefing session. For example, some people will like a detailed and logical step-by-step approach to the task, while others will like a quick overview of what they need to do. Some people will like a briefing document in writing in advance of your meeting, while others will like an informal conversation about the task and its relative importance to the organisation.

Whatever the personality type of the person you select, there is an appropriate style of communication that will produce better results in a more time-efficient manner. Take a little time to pick up on the clues that identify different personality types and this will improve your delegation effectiveness. Choose the communication style that suits the delegate, and not your preferred style of communicating.

Step 3: Brief the delegate and gain task acceptance

Don't rush in with orders to do this or that. Invest your time in clearly briefing the delegate – time can easily be lost when you delegate a vague task to someone. Assumptions are made and results therefore vary. Never use imprecise statements like, 'Whenever you get the chance, would you complete this task for me?' or, 'Do it the way you think is best.' These types of instructions will lead to various interpretations of what you really want. Your briefing of the delegate is about bringing clarity to your

'Whatever the role, proper briefing is essential – you cannot hold people responsible for vague or undefined tasks.'

Robert Heller

instructions. Explain exactly what you want done, why it is necessary to pass on this task to them, and when you need the task completed.

A simple but effective way to bring clarity to the task you wish to delegate is to write your brief using the SMARTER Way Goal Setting System™ as discussed in the first chapter. It forces you to be specific, with a measurement for success clearly stated. It also defines a clear timescale for completion and focuses on the motivation for the delegate, which will ensure a sense of commitment. Writing out your briefing document doesn't take long and it is a valuable use of time as it gets everyone onto the same page. Both parties will see the task in its entirety and what is involved in its successful completion. It will eliminate assumptions and surprises.

A good briefing session is about more than just passing on a task. It will also free up some thinking time if used effectively. Masters of time use this briefing session to stimulate their colleagues to think for themselves. They know that mental time can take up even more time than the task itself so they also want to delegate the mental side of the task. They achieve this by asking delegates challenging, open, and probing questions around how they think the task should be tackled, what issues may arise and how they would solve them, what options are available to complete the task and what steps they will take to get the job done. This joint approach frees up additional time and forges greater commitment to the task and to the delegation process.

Finally, the briefing session is about making sure the delegate is clear about what they are responsible for and what their deadline is. It can act as an informal agreement between you and the delegate. Finish your briefing session, depending on their personality type, with: 'Are you comfortable taking on this task?' or, 'Will you be able to deliver on time to the agreed standard?' This will gauge willingness and the acceptance of the task by the delegate.

Step 4: Provide support to the delegate
It is important to emphasise that you need results and performance to the agreed standard, not excuses or problems. You are there to provide support and it is in both of your interests that the tasks are successfully completed. Delegation is not about dumping your workload on someone else.

The level of support required should be agreed up front as this will eliminate feelings of being left alone or too closely monitored. Supporting your colleagues effectively will build trust and encourage them to extend themselves. You will create an environment where people build their skill-sets and are willing to take on more tasks, which frees up even more time for you. The right level of support ensures no one feels exploited. Instead there is a feeling of being able to use their full range of skills.

This opportunity to develop a colleague was clearly missed by John when Craig asked him if he could help with the sales report. Instead of investing some time in training Craig, he simply closed down another avenue of help available to him. No wonder John is clocking up the hours he works each week. John failed to align his needs to what Craig offered. Masters of time seek out opportunities to delegate and rarely pass up openings such as the one presented to John.

Step 5: Control task performance

It is good practice to establish some checkpoints, which will monitor the progress of the delegated task. Control is a vital factor in ensuring the delegation process actually saves you time overall. It is important this control system is approved by both parties upfront; there is a fine line between good control and interference. You need to control the progress of the task to ensure its completion on time and to the agreed standard. Too much control means you don't save yourself any time because you spend most of it monitoring instead of doing other important tasks. Too little control potentially means tasks take up to twice as much of your time as you end up doing them anyway.

A good control system will provide you with the opportunity to efficiently monitor the progress of delegated tasks and to identify and resolve any problems in a timely manner. The purpose of your control system is not only to ensure the tasks get completed to the agreed standard but also that you save time by delegating. Your control system should be linked to your support system, and also tied into maintaining the will of the delegate. Monitoring the progress of the tasks will provide you with numerous opportunities to praise the work of the delegate.

> 'Recognition is so easy to do and so inexpensive to distribute, there is simply no excuse for not doing it... Recognition signifies someone noticed and someone cares.'
> Rosabeth Moss Kanter

Step 6: Debrief the delegate

The final stage in the delegating process is the debriefing session. This is often overlooked, which results in more time-wastage the next time you delegate this task. There is a lot of vital learning for both sides in a frank and honest debriefing session. The results from this session can be incorporated into your brief for the next time you have to delegate to someone, which will enable you to do a better job of planning and authorising future tasks.

Within 24 hours of the delegated task being completed you should get together with the delegate for your debriefing session. This session will help you gauge the initial reactions, frustrations, challenges, likes and dislikes of the delegate to the task. You should also evaluate whether you gave them enough support and guidance, and if it would have really been quicker if you did it yourself.

Keep the meeting short and focused on establishing some key learning points. Explain the purpose of the session so that the environment of open and honest communication can take place. Start the debriefing session with some general questions, such as:

What was the performance standard achieved? Encourage the delegate to outline their assessment of their performance. Although ultimate responsibility remains with you for the task completion, you want the delegate to be accountable for their work. If there was a below-standard performance, establish the cause and solution so that it can be rectified the next time.

How did the delegate feel about taking on the task, and how did they feel after it was completed? This will help you to identify the delegate's commitment to the task and whether or not they are willing to take it on again.

What changes could be implemented to improve the performance? There will always be lessons learnt after you have completed a task. Identify the ones that will save you time on the next occasion you have to delegate. Small changes can sometimes save you a lot of time.

How well was the delegate briefed initially? Did they understand the full parameters of the task? This is an opportunity to review your communication skills. Establish whether you appealed to their communication style or not. Ask them how they would have approached the briefing session. Identify if there were any gaps in the task's description, note any omissions, and update your briefing document.

How much time did you save by delegating the task? Conduct a quick time-benefit analysis to establish if it is worth delegating this task again. Remember the main purpose of this process is to save yourself time, which you can then use to add real value to your day.

What would you do differently the next time? Summarise the key lessons learnt from this process and implement the changes the next time you delegate.

Keep the debriefing session on track; each session should be short and to the point, otherwise you could end up wasting a lot of time meandering off on a tangent. It is your responsibility to keep the delegate focused on providing information on how the delegating process worked for you both and what improvement, if any, you can include in the process the next time.

Delegating is not static: as your team and individuals develop, so too will the way you delegate. Use the skill/will matrix to help you adapt your strategy to meet the needs of the person who will get the tasks done for you.

Is it working for you?

Delegation is a great way of saving time. Masters of time are highly skilled delegators. They make a decision to delegate a task and proceed without delay. This ensures that they maximise the time benefit of delegating. Indecision wastes time.

Analyse the progress you are making to ensure delegation works for you over a period of time. Track the number of times you delegate during the day. Calculate the number of hours your delegation policy has now recovered for you. Analyse the cost of delegating verses the rewards gained. Then answer this simple question: Are these recovered hours now being used to add real value to you and your organisation?

'Leaders make decisions, and momentum in business is based on decision-making, not sitting on your hands.'

Allan Leighton

INTRODUCING MASTER OF TIME TO THE HOME

You are a slave to the clock, creating an environment where the role you have at work and the role you have at home are unbalanced. Series of appointments, the endless fight against deadlines, trying to get the most out of your day and setting challenging goals are the principles by which you live your life. You measure success by ensuring every minute of every day is accounted for and is productive. There is intense guilt if you are idle for a moment. You seek perfection and therefore you find

'A successful life is one that is lived through understanding and pursuing one's own path, not chasing after the dreams of others.'

Chin-Ning Chu

Dos and don'ts of delegation

Do: Be a master
- Organise your workload
- Create a habit of delegating
- Practise your skills of delegating
- Focus on the process for delegating
- Regularly review your results and analyse the amount of time you recover by delegating tasks

Don't: Be a slave
- Blame others for your poor use of time
- Allow mistrust to prevent you from delegating
- Be penny wise and pound foolish with your time
- Dump your work on others
- Refuse help from colleagues
- Fail to learn from previous delegating experiences

delegating impossible. You live your life based on the expectations of others. You are under pressure to do more in less time.

Taking on more and more tasks means you spend less time on the things you should be focusing on and will end up regretting wasted time. Harry Chapin's classic song 'Cat in the Cradle' tells the story of a father who is too busy to spend time with his son: despite pleas from the boy, he always has an excuse and promises that one day he'll have some time to play with him. Unfortunately, the father never finds the time, and years later the boy turns the tables on his aging father. The last verse ends with the lines, 'I'd love to, Dad, if I could find the time / You see my new job's a hassle and the kids have the flu / But it's sure nice talking to you, Dad… And as I hung up the phone, it occurred to me / He'd grown up just like me / My boy was just like me'. You need a balance between work and home life before work becomes your life. You need to find ways to re-energise yourself by spending quality time doing the things that matter most to you. Create space for an alternative to the challenging demands of your work life.

Masters of time are doing what they want with their lives, achieving the goals they set themselves on their own terms. They spend enough time with the people they love, doing the things that inspire them, and are constantly working towards their vision of freedom, happiness and success. They share the workload that goes into running a home. They have learnt the art of delegating, which ensures there is enough time to spend on the activities that are of value to them. They are passionate about maintaining a balance in the roles they play between work and home. Anne Mcgee-Cooper believes this balance also brings a lot of energy, which allows people to achieve more with their time. She says, 'Along with passion, the most important and undergriding element of high-energy living seems to be balance. Learning to live in balance, allowing time for both work and a rewarding personal life, will bring synergy, joy, enthusiasm and creativity to your life.'

Teaching others to take on some of your workload is a great way of spending quality time with people who are special to you. Whether it is your children, family or friends, delegating tasks can be fun and rewarding for both parties. At home, delegating should be about getting things done together and with enthusiasm. Masters of time are high achievers both in work and at home. They use the same strategy for success, which is to complete the important tasks and not just the urgent tasks. They know when it is time to delegate routine jobs to the right people. Instead of spending Saturday mornings cleaning windows, washing the car and doing general DIY jobs, they outsource these tasks, which allows them to spend time bringing their children to their various sport activities. Instead of cleaning the house and ironing, they again outsource these labour-intensive jobs, which again frees up a lot time they then spend on family activities.

Making delegation fun and exciting at home will bring balance to your life. It requires the same discipline of planning, organising and co-ordination you apply in the workplace. Follow the process and free up some valuable time. Managing yourself at home with the same dedication as you manage yourself in work is an important step in your journey to a positive work-life balance. Identify the routine jobs you can delegate and then start a new habit of delegating these jobs to family members or outsource them to local service providers or teenagers looking to earn some pocket money.

Before you read any further, take a break and write down the next part of your plan.

'The big secret in life is that there is no big secret. Whatever your goal, you can get there if you're willing to work.'

Oprah Winfrey

PERSONAL THOUGHTS

What will I do differently tomorrow?

MYTH NO. 7
THE OFFICE IS TOO NOISY

BUSINESS MANAGEMENT SKILLS – ORGANISING

John works in a typical cubicle environment. Invented in the 1960s by Bob Probst, a professor of fine arts at the University of Colorado, the cubicle has become associated with office buildings. It was originally designed so that office workers could freely discuss and trade ideas without having to leave their desks. However, this classic cubicle is a breeding ground for slaves to the clock. It contains all the ingredients slaves thrive on. It's noisy, full of time-wasting distractions, and overcrowded with other slaves. No wonder its inventor grew to despise it.

John has a unique filing system. His desk is piled high with files, yellow and pink notes are stuck all over his PC screen, and long to-do lists are pinned to his noticeboard. You are also likely to find an array of jumble items, ranging from old coffee mugs with funny sayings on them to year-old magazines; old notebooks containing half-completed to-do lists, a constant reminder of the tasks he failed to do; and bits of paper with telephone numbers and a first name beside them, surnames long forgotten. His work area is a cluttered mess, which hinders his ability to produce timely reports and work output. It looks unprofessional. His clutter makes it hard to concentrate on any one activity at a time as every item in the mess screams out, 'Look at me, look at me.'

No wonder John finds it difficult to meet his deadlines. His working environment is a catalogue of distractions and poor working principles. He spends hours each day looking for items that are missing because of the clutter. Even the cleaner refuses to clean his work space.

'The greatest glory in living lies not in never falling, but in rising every time we fall.'

Nelson Mandela

Get organised

There is a link between clutter and slave-like behaviour. Some psychologists believe a cluttered desk displays a deep-rooted problem with making decisions and planning. People with a large amount of clutter find it difficult to decide what goes and what stays. They fail to create space for new things that could be more beneficial to them. The lack of space is due largely to a non-existent planning and filing system. As the clutter grows and multiplies so does the amount of time wasted – it slows you down by making it harder for you to find the items you need.

Slaves to the clock should recognise that there is a link between their cluttered working environment and their cluttered work schedule. Julie Morgenstern writes in *Time Management from the Inside Out* that you need to change your perception of time and view it as something tangible. She links time to clutter and feels you can master time by using the same skills that you use to master clutter. She writes, 'In my own journey to getting organised, my biggest breakthrough came when I realised that organising time is no different than organising space.' Compare a cluttered closet to a cluttered schedule.

Cluttered closet	Cluttered schedule
Limited amount of space	Limited amount of hours
Crammed with more things than storage space allows	Crammed with more tasks than time allows
Items jammed into any available pocket of space, in no particular order	Tasks jammed into any available pocket of time, in no particular order
Haphazard arrangement makes it difficult to see what you have	Haphazard arrangement makes it difficult to see what you have to do
Inefficient in its use of organising tools	Inefficient in its use of time management tools

You may be thinking that improving how you use your time has nothing to do with how organised your desk is, but you can use the same skills you use to de-clutter and organise your wardrobe, garage or kitchen. You can create a working environment that eliminates many of the time-wasting activities that drag you down. Start with your desk and devise a clear-desk policy that works for you. The benefits of this clear-desk policy include:

- A place for everything and everything is in its place, so you spend less time looking for important items
- A clear, orderly desk gives you a clear, orderly mind, which frees up mental space. This allows you to think in a clear way
- A professional image
- A more flexible approach to work
- Gives more energy as you lose that feeling of being bogged down with too much baggage

Breaking free from the office clutter trap

Many books have been written about clutter, its effects and how to sort out the mess. They will provide you with great ideas and information. Examine what the term clutter means to you. Clutter, according to the *Collins Dictionary*, means 'untidy mess'. Other words associated with clutter include confusion, disarray, disorder, litter and muddle. These words do not send out positive messages and they certainly do not paint a picture of professionalism. How many hours do you spend looking for things every day?

If your world is full of clutter, you are allowing yourself to be weighed down with excessive baggage. Unwanted clutter is a reminder of the past, your past life that is stopping you from moving on. It prevents you from developing your career. James A. Belasco and Ralph C. Stayer in *Flight of the Buffalo* talk about the need to ruthlessly deal with non-value activities. They explain, 'A lot of non-essential activities, like weeds, grow up in every organisation. They did in mine. I learned to attack them vigorously and consistently, and enlist everyone else to join in the attack.'

They achieved their goal by getting back to the basics. They started the process by listing all the activities in their company. They soon realised that, like other slaves to the clock, they had gained many non-essential items over the years because no one asked the right questions. 'What does this activity contribute to the bottom line? What would happen if we didn't do it anymore?' The answer to these two simple but challenging questions had a major impact on their business, not only in saving time but also on the overall costs to the business: they found ways to reduce costs by 37 per cent. Today is a great time to start your personal weeding-out programme.

'Out of clutter find simplicity; from discord find harmony; in the middle of difficulty lies opportunity.'
Albert Einstein

Master your time

What non-essential task will you get rid of today?

Breaking free from the clutter trap in your work space

Now that you have started the process, it is time to manage clutter in your work space. You must work within your company's rules – there may be some items you would like to get rid of, but your company needs to retain them. So, before dumping any company items check first. For example, never throw out old customer files unless you are authorised to do so as you may require them for compliance reasons. One possibility might be to store them in the general store area instead.

However, you can still be ruthless when it comes to your personal belongings, especially with your locker and personal cabinets. For some reason these are the breeding ground for old shoes and uniforms, gym gear and party clothes, not to mention out-of-date brochures and stationery. The strategy here is simple: use it, store it or dump it.

Once your locker is cleaned out, which will take a lot less time than you would imagine (you might have wasted more time thinking about it than actually doing it), it is time to work on your desk. For every item ask this question: Do I need this item to do the task I'm currently working on? If yes, it stays; if no, it is put back into its place until you need it. Pack away any inactive items in a clearly labelled box and put them into storage. This simple exercise will ensure there are no distractions on your desk.

If you suffer from the yellow-sticker disease (PC and walls covered in little reminder notes all screaming at you), then the medicine is simple. Take them all down and either put the information into your contacts listing, include it on your adding-value list, or discard. Yellow stickers are a distraction and not helpful reminders. Remove all of them today.

As your working space starts to de-clutter, you will begin to feel more energised and can now focus on getting important tasks completed. Simplify your work station. Excessive clutter needs to be managed so that you can work in an environment that is professional and devoid of potential time-wasting distractions.

Noise pollution

Working environments, especially open-plan offices, are full of noise pollution, which is a major cause of time-wastage. Noise will interrupt your thinking as well as prevent you from doing your work. Noise pollution takes many different forms, including:

Mobile phone ring-tones. Personalised ring-tones may be amusing to some people but can be very irritating to others, particularly in the work environment. They can be loud and will distract people.

Teleconferencing in a shared office. A modern way to communicate with people in various locations, it also saves travel time. However, in an open-plan environment a conference call (on speakers) will interrupt the rest of the office.

Loud, extroverted people. They burst into the office full of the joys of spring. They are ready to talk to their colleagues on the way to their desks. Their cheeriness can be infectious, but they will create noise that will interrupt everyone. These distractions may not be welcomed by all staff.

The radio. Switch it off, even if it is only playing soft background music. You will find yourself singing along to your favourite song and losing your concentration. Talk shows are even worse because an interesting topic will come on just as you begin an important task. Also, take your neighbours into consideration, because the radio could be distracting them.

Coffee machine. If your desk is near the water cooler or coffee station, move either your desk or the drinks machine. Otherwise you will be constantly interrupted directly or indirectly by your colleagues' chit-chat. You will get sucked into their conversations and lose valuable time.

Who controls the noise?
People talk about noise pollution in their office in the same way they talk about pollution in the environment. It is always someone else who is causing it. They make statements like, 'I can't do anything about all the talking that goes on around me,' or, 'I wish they would turn off their mobile phones or at least change that irritating ring-tone.'

This way of thinking compounds the situation, as it implies you are a victim with no power to change your situation. It is also an easy get-out clause because you don't have to take responsibility to reduce the noise. If the noise is affecting you, then you must manage the situation. One approach is to politely but assertively explain to the noise polluter the effect their noise is having on you and suggest a course of action.

Dos and don'ts of getting rid of clutter

Do: Be a master
- Create space for new things
- Future focus
- Simplify your work station
- Use it, store it or dump it

Don't: Be a slave
- Waste time looking for things lost in the clutter
- Get weighed down by excessive baggage
- Gain non-essential items

When was the last time you did this?

Complete a full survey of your home:

- List all the minor jobs that need completing in each room
- Consult a local handyperson and get an estimate for the repair work
- Schedule each job
- Agree who will do what
- Make it happen

INTRODUCING MASTER OF TIME TO THE HOME

Moll Anderson talks about moving forward with your life by simply 'getting rid of all that old stuff you're storing in the attic of your mind'. Your untidy mess is an accumulation of possessions that have no place in your future happiness. This is not about the few items that bring you happy memories – the possessions that create clutter are old boxes full of Christmas and birthday cards, piles of old newspapers and magazines, shoes and clothes that will never be worn again, books that will never be read and gym equipment that will never be used.

If your house is so full of clutter that the attic is overflowing with redundant belongings, every wardrobe and press is stuffed to capacity, the shed and garage require mountaineering skills to reach the ladder on the back wall, and the spare bedroom has become a dumping ground no one dares enter for safety reasons, then take this advice: chuck it all out now. It is not a healthy or fun way to live.

It is also important to note that getting rid of your clutter is not the same as doing a 'spring cleaning' job. That's clearing the mess and making your home tidy. Getting rid of clutter is an ongoing process. It should be built into your weekly cleaning routine. As new items come in, ensure something else leaves. Remember the golden rule: 'Getting rid of clutter is getting rid of the obstacles that prevent you from moving on.' Pin this rule to the inside of your cleaning cupboard to remind you before you do your cleaning. If you haven't found a use for something in the last twelve months, chances are you won't use it in the next twelve months.

Some day I'll get around to it

Another form of clutter you need to get rid of around the house is that great source of conflict and loss of valuable time – the unfinished DIY job. DIY stands for do-it-yourself; unfortunately they forgot to add 'if you have the skills, time and real desire'. These unsightly, unfinished and definitely undesirable blotches drain your energy and are constant reminders of your own imperfections.

The list is endless: the leaky pipes that lead to black damp patches, the unfinished paints jobs that resemble the morning after the night before, the broken hinge that leaves the door resting like the arm of a well-oiled drunk draped over a counter, the cracked glass that mirrors your fragile state of mind, and on and on it goes. The longer the list, the more you get depressed about it. Slaves to the clock tend to spend more time thinking about these jobs than actually doing them. You will be surprised how cheap it is to get the repairs carried out by a professional.

I didn't think they were so beautiful

Turning your home into a clutter-free zone will not only free up more space but also show off your most highly prized possessions in their fullest beauty. You will rediscover lost gems, perhaps hidden under a pile of worn-out clothes or dusty books and magazines. You will be surprised how attractive things can look when they are given enough space.

Starting the clutter-free process

There is no time like the present to start the clutter-free process. Invest an hour a day or two hours over the weekend. Put on your ruthless hat and complete one room at a time. Make a list of all the items that make you feel good, that have a real purpose or function, or that are beautiful. Everything thing else can go. If they don't make the list, they go. Send them to the dump, give them away to someone who really needs them, or pop down to the local charity shop, where you will be welcomed with open arms. Or, you can always go to a car boot sale and try and sell your unwanted and unloved possessions there. Starting your clutter-free campaign is as simple as that.

When it comes to your clothes, pick out all the outfits that make you look and feel good. Always apply the 'dress good feel good' rule to your wardrobe, even when choosing your lounging-around clothes. No cast-offs allowed. Anything that is out of style, looks shabby or you haven't worn in some time makes the 'on the way to the charity shop' list. These clothes will only hinder your feel-good image. The same clinical approach applies to your shoes and all other accessories.

Your junk room, whether it is a spare bedroom or garage, should become a proper storage area. Any item that is broken gets repaired immediately, otherwise you dump it. Install a proper storage system. Invest in a good shelving unit. Storage boxes should either be see-through or have labels attached to make identification of the contents easier. This will save you hours looking for items.

Less clutter leaves more free space both in the home and the mind and helps you to spend your time doing the things that really matter. It brings more energy to your life.

Before you read any further, take a break and write down the next part of your plan.

Healthy home options

Books
Buy one, sell one

Clothes
If you haven't worn it this year chuck it out (recycle)

Magazines
When read get rid of

Toys
If your children don't play with them, give them to some children who will

Gym equipment
Work out or throw out

Garage/shed
Storage for tools and equipment you use; it is not a junk yard

'Never again clutter your days or nights with so many menial and unimportant things that you have no time to accept a real challenge when it comes along. This applies to play as well as work. A day merely survived is no cause for celebration. You are not here to fritter away your precious hours when you have the ability to accomplish so much by making a slight change in your routine. No more busy work. No more hiding from success. Leave time, leave space, to grow. Now. Now! Not tomorrow!'

Og Mandino

PERSONAL THOUGHTS

What will I do differently tomorrow?

YESTERDAY A SLAVE TO THE CLOCK, TODAY A MASTER OF TIME

BUSINESS MANAGEMENT SKILLS – CO-ORDINATING

John, like so many people today, has reached a crossroads in his life. He has been a slave to the clock for longer than he would care to remember. His slave-like behaviour not only affects him but also those around him. His failure to meet deadlines infuriates his boss, Alex, and shows him in a bad light with his colleagues. Failing to delegate highlights his distinct lack of trust in his colleagues and his unwillingness to develop his team. He knows he must prioritise his workload, but he allows interruptions to play havoc with his cluttered schedule. He is constantly fire-fighting because of his lack of foresight to plan effectively.

His desk is a mess and he wastes much of his time looking for important items. Perhaps even more is spent worrying that his cluttered desk is a symbol of his poor decision-making skills. He runs haphazardly from one meeting to another, taking on more tasks, leaving less time available to complete existing ones. It is time for a change and for John to take responsibility for his plight so that he can become a master of time.

The next 60 minutes will change his life as John finally understands the underlying principle about time management: manage yourself and those around and let time take care of itself. Seek out every opportunity to add value to your life.

Blame culture versus responsibility culture

Managing your life is your responsibility. Slave-like behaviour is rampant in a blame culture. Slaves to the clock fail to take responsibility for their

> 'Change is the law of life. And those who look only to the past or present are certain to miss the future.'
>
> John F. Kennedy

> 'No man is fit to command another that cannot command himself.'
>
> William Penn

125

behaviour. They believe there isn't enough time to complete their tasks, although their colleagues seem to be able to finish on time. They prefer to blame their colleagues for not knowing how to do a task rather than spend time teaching them. They feel they are controlled by their circumstances rather than in control of them. If something goes wrong, they will waste more time trying to establish who is to blame rather than spending time ensuring it won't happen again. In short, blame culture wastes time.

Shifting from blame culture and building trust requires people to take responsibility. It is an important step in becoming a master of time. It is your time; you are responsible for its use. A master of time takes responsibility to turn their vision statement into their living world, to turn nagging to-do lists into adding-value lists of tasks they want to do. They know how they really spend their precious time; they control the volume of interruptions; they only attend adding-value meetings; they delegate as much as possible; and they create the environment that is right for them to perform at an optimum level.

Choose the right path

Being a master of time is a way of life. It is more than taking a few time management tips and techniques and believing they will improve your time management skills. It is about being brave and choosing the right path.

> Alice came to a fork in the road.
> 'Which road do I take?' she asked.
> 'Where do you want to go?' responded the Cheshire cat.
> 'I don't know,' Alice answered.
> 'Then,' said the cat, 'it doesn't matter.'
>
> Lewis Carroll, *Alice in Wonderland*

It requires a vision of what you want to do with your time and dedication, and commitment to turning this vision into your way of life. Greatness doesn't come easy but can be achieved by those who know what they want. Take a moment and think about how you can inspire yourself to greatness.

Write a poster

Creating a poster is an excellent way to visually capture your strategy for becoming a master of time. It is your advertisement to the world that you intend to become a master of time. Your poster can contain your vision statement, some inspiring quotes to maintain your motivation, your SMARTER goals and your top five slave-like behaviours you will eliminate from your life. The poster should be bright and inspiring. Display your personal poster in a prominent area so that it will grab people's attention. You want it to convey your strategy, its importance to you and the organisation, and the role that others can play in helping you become a master of time. It is a fun way to show people you are serious about changing the way you manage your life.

Maintain commitment to the journey

Starting your journey, although daunting at first, is the easy part. Maintaining your desire to continually build on your vision requires talent, conviction that you are on the right road, and persistence.

In an effort to improve how you use your time, it is easy to implement a solution to one of your slave-like behaviours and then allow the solution to outlive its usefulness and become part of the problem. To avoid this scenario and to maintain your driving force, you should write a weekly 4/15 report on Friday afternoon. The report is brief, asks four key questions and shouldn't take more than 15 minutes to complete. The four questions are:

- What did I achieve this week that adds value to being a master of time?
- Have any old habits returned?
- Are any new habits out of date?
- What are my SMARTER goals for next week?

Reread this report on Monday and deal with any issues before the end of the next week. This 15-minute habit will keep you on track and in control of your strategy for managing yourself and those around you.

It's time to break free

The bottom line is that there are many myths around time management, which are the cause for so many people becoming slaves to the clock. People who look for the easy option to improve their time management skills by following a few old reliable tips and techniques will remain slaves to the clock. These tips have been around for years and have failed to deliver.

To become a master of time requires a major mind shift. Stephen Covey believes that what is needed is:

Dos and don'ts

Do: Be a master

- Understand you cannot manage time, you must manage yourself and those around you and let time take care of itself
- Choose the correct path for you
- Write an inspiring poster to advertise your journey
- Turn tips and techniques into winning habits

Don't: Be a slave

- Wait for the right moment to start, it never arrives
- Blame everyone else for being a slave to the clock
- Start well but fade quickly
- Use old time management tips and techniques and expect major improvements

More than an evolution, we need a revolution. We need to move beyond time management to life leadership – to a fourth generation based on paradigms that will create quality-of-life results.

The quality of your time management skills is shaped by your personality, attitude and behaviours. A change in your mind shift can be accomplished by doing the following:

- Create your vision for your life
- Use SMARTER goals to turn this vision into a way of life
- Conduct a time audit to understand how you really spend your time as opposed to how you think you use your time
- Prioritise the important things in your life and not just the urgent things
- Compose adding-value lists and not nagging to-do lists
- Take responsibility for controlling the volume of non-value interruptions stealing your time
- Attend value-adding meeting only
- Free up some time by delegating as much as possible
- Turn a messy environment into a productive, clutter-free zone

TOP TIPS FROM THE BUSINESS WORLD

The challenge here is to turn these tips into habits that will help you become a master of time; they all work and have been successfully implemented by the people below who work in similar business environments to yours. Transform these tips into winning daily habits and over time they will improve your performance.

> My top tip to deal with new tasks is to 'handle a piece of paper once'. By the time you spend reading the document, understanding it, prioritising it and then deciding whether you want to deal with it now or later, you can be halfway through the process. If you leave it to one side, it will always remain in the back of your mind as unfinished work, adding to your stress and reducing your concentration on the task at hand. The trick is to leave a window to tackle these unknown tasks and then use that time effectively.
>
> Brian Kavanagh, financial services sector

Delegate it.

> The simple philosophy of a highly successful managing
> director in the media business

Handle a piece of paper only once.

> Anne Brady, accountancy sector

My top tip would be, 'If it is rubbish, bin it.' This would apply to e-mails, mail shots, letters and other correspondence you receive. You have to have an aggressive filtering system in place to sort out what is high and low priority and what relates and does not relate to you. If it not relevant – bin it.'

> Brendan Gillen, finance operations, third-level education

No magic formula springs to mind – I just write a list every day!

> Colm Begley, training and development sector

The best time management tip, which I use every day, is as follows. Each task I receive is given the 3D treatment – I either:

> Do it – Task must be completed by me
> Delegate it – Task can/should be done by a team member
> Dump it – No value in completing task

> Rory O'Hare, health insurance sector

A lot of my time mis-management (potentially) is the constant stream of e-mails received. So, a bit like the old time management books that said 'only handle each piece of paper once', I adhere to the principle of that with e-mails. So, I only open an e-mail when I'm ready to deal with it, I deal with it, and then I delete it.

> Brendan Spring, financial service sector

Here are my top three tips:

1. Set a weekly handwritten to-do list with not more than four 'criticals' at the top. Don't use Outlook Task Manager to remind you.
2. My favourite: The first 60 seconds at your desk set the tone for the day. Identify your top two priorities for the day and plan when you will get them done. Enter it into your diary/ organiser. Do this task before you switch your PC on or check e-mails on your Blackberry.
3. Delegate the small things.

> David Storrs, learning and management training sector

Take the time to use your e-mail out of office, to make people aware of your status. The volume of mail you receive will drop substantially, whilst the quality will increase!

Dean Anderson

My only tip is to stick to your diary – rigidly – no excuses. Enter the most important things you have got to do/commit to others to do and then discipline yourself to stick to it come hell or high water – this in turns means that anything you put into your diary gets done!

Jimmy Ambrose, financial services sector

My top tip for time management is to 'eat your frog for breakfast' – basically, if you've got something unpleasant to do, get it over with as soon as you can, otherwise the thought of having to do it will consume more energy and time than the actual doing of it!

Martin Downes, management and technology consultancy

My tip is to spend a few minutes at the end of each day reviewing what you need to accomplish the following day, make your list and then prioritise. It means that you start your working day with a sense of purpose and structure.

Michele Ryan, human resources

- Keep a diary of calls, especially when busy, so return calls and follow-ups do not get forgotten
- Plan out a schedule for your week ahead and review this list on a daily basis for a few minutes to keep on eye on your progress
- Leave an afternoon at the end of each week free for catching up
- Limit meetings to one in the morning and one in the afternoon to allow for running-over time at any meeting without disrupting all plans for the rest of your day
- Last thing each evening, clear your desk so you feel you're starting each day fresh in the morning

Deirdre Connolly, graphic and website design

My top tip and one that does make a difference is to set your daily agenda the night before. This way, you arrive into the office with all your tasks, appointments, etc. laid out in front of you.

Garret Buckley, events and exhibitions

- Plan tomorrow today – at the end of each day take five minutes to prioritise the next day
- Plan next week at end of this week – at the end of the week plan the week ahead
- Plan next month at the end of this month – take 20 minutes to look at the month ahead and set deadlines for what you want to achieve by the end of the month
- Look ahead to the next three months – what's on the horizon – plan in time now to deal with it
- Watch for elephants – on the horizon they look pretty small, but be careful you don't end up with an elephant foot in your cereal bowl!

Kate Marshall, learning and management development

My two favourite tips are:

1. When away from the office, on return sort your e-mail by subject and read only the most recent mail – you can then decide to delete previous mails on the same subject.
2. Always start your day by dealing with the most difficult task that the day presents first – once accomplished, the rest of the day is downhill.

Neil Kelly, banking sector

This phrase always comes to mind when I think of time management: 'Time is always managed (either poorly or well); repeat this at your busiest and quietest time of the day and it will add awareness to your time management actions.'

Jonny Miller, learning and management development

Philip E. Atkinson, in his book *Achieving Results through Time Management*, identifies the 15 minutes before lunch as a good time for procrastinators to start a task. He writes

Make the 15 minutes before lunch work for you. Ensure that you devote those 15 minutes to specific action. This may mean writing a report. You may start and have completed half a page before lunchtime – this is usually time when you would be winding down, talking to others.

Now that you have finished reading, it is time pull all of your great ideas together and summarise them into your personal plan for becoming a true master of time. What will be the first and last step of your journey?

If you take your eyes off your goals you will only see the barriers, and if you stop listening to your heart you will only hear negative thoughts. Be strong, be brave, be visionary, be happy, be a master of time.

PERSONAL THOUGHTS

What is the first step you will take tomorrow?

What will be your final step?

BIBLIOGRAPHY

Adair, John, *The Skills of Leadership* (Gower Publishing Company Ltd).

Anderson, Moll, *Change Your Home, Change Your Life* (Thomas Nelson, 2006).

Atkinson, Philip E, *Achieving Results through Time Management* (Pitman Publishing, 1988).

Belasco, James A., and Stayer, Ralph C., *Flight of the Buffalo* (Warner Books, 1994).

Blanchard, Ken, and Stoner, Jesse, *Full Steam Ahead* (Berrett–Kochler Publishers Inc., 2004).

Bowles, Susan, 'Trim the fat from office meetings', *USA Today* (11/12/2002).

Cadbury, Sir Adrian, *The Company Chairman* (Director Books, 1990).

Cagen, Sasha, *To-Do List: From Buying Milk to Finding a Soulmate, What Our Lists Reveal About Us* (Fireside, 2007).

Cialdini, Robert B., *Influence: The Psychology of Persuasion* (Collins, 2006).

Covey, Stephen, *The Seven Habits of Highly Effective People* (Simon & Schuster, 1989).

Gallagher, B.J., and Ventura, Steve, *Who Are 'They' Anyway?* (Kaplan Business, 2004).

Gates, Bill, 'The Wright Brothers: The 100 most important people of the century', *Time* (29/03/1999).

Gates, Bill, *Business @ the Speed of Thought* (Warner Books, 2000).

Griessman, Eugene, *Time Tactics of Very Successful People* (McGraw–Hill, 1994).

Harrington, Padraig, *Journey to the Open* (Bantam Press, 2007).

Heller, Robert, *How to Delegate* (DK Publishing, 1998).

Hendrickson, Elisabeth, 'The tyranny of the "to do" list', *Sticky Minds* (31/10/2005).

James, William, *The Principles of Psychology* (Harvard, 1890).

Kelley, Robert E., *How to Be a STAR at Work* (Random House, 1998).

Kennedy, Mary, *Lines I Love* (Merlin Publishing, 2007).

Lennon, Neil, *Man and Bhoy* (HarperCollins, 2007).

MacKenzie, R. Alex, *The Time Trap: The Classic Book on Time Management* (MJF Books, 2002).

McCarthy, Barbara, 'Ireland: Hey, we're trying to do some work here', *The Sunday Times* (5/2/2006).

McGrath, Paul, *Back from the Brink* (Century, 2006).

McGee-Cooper, Anne, *You Don't Have to Go Home from Work Exhausted! A Program to Bring Joy, Energy and Balance to Your Life* (Bantam Books, 1992).

McGirt, Ellen, 'Getting out from under', *Fortune Magazine* (15/3/2006).

Machowicz, Richard J., *Unleash the Warrior Within* (Marlowe & Company, 2002).

Morgenstern, Julie, *Time Management from the Inside Out* (Henry Holt, 2000).

Parker, Glenn, and Hoffman, Robert, *Meeting Excellence: 33 Tools to Lead Meetings that Get Results* (Jossey–Bass, 2006).

Parkinson, C. Northcote, 'Parkinson's Law: The pursuit of progress', *The Economist* (1955).

Peters, Tom, and Waterman, Robert, *In Search of Excellence* (HarperCollins, 1995).

Prone, Terry, and Lyons, Kieran, *This Business of Writing* (ICAI, 2006).

Rosman, Katherine, 'The way we list now', *The Wall Street Journal.*

Rotella, Dr Bob, *Golf is Not a Game of Perfect* (Simon & Schuster, 1995).

Sandberg, Jared, 'Though time-consuming, to-do lists are a way of life', *The Wall Street Journal* (10/09/2004).

Sloan Jr, Alfred P., *My Years with General Motors* (Diane Pub Co., 1990).

Smedley, Tim, ' "Alpha Mail" An article about Allan Leighton', *People Management* (20/9/2007).

Smith, Hyrum W., *The Ten Natural Laws of Successful Time and Life Management* (Business Plus, 1995).

Snair, Scott, *Stop the Meeting I Want to Get Off* (McGraw–Hill, 2003).

Streibel, Barbara J., *Plan and Conduct Effective Meetings – 24 Steps to Generate Meaningful Results* (McGraw–Hill, 2007).

Tyler, Kathryn, 'Evaluate your next move: Regular audits of your strategic HR business plan help keep your department on track', 2001 Society for Human Resource Management & 2001 Gale Group.

Wilde, Oscar, *Lady Windermere's Fan* from *Oscar Wilde – The Major Works* (Oxford, 2000).